Toward an International Criminal Court?

Three Options

Presented as

Presidential Speeches

Alton Frye, Project Director

A Council Policy Initiative

Sponsored by the Council on Foreign Relations

Speech One: Endorse the International Criminal Court

It is not difficult to see why these mass murderers regularly escape justice. In many countries, prosecutors and judges enjoy no independence. A late-night phone call or an intimidating visit is frequently all it takes to discourage investigation or prosecution of official crimes. As added insurance, many tyrants decree amnesties for themselves to make it legally difficult to pursue their crimes.

As we look to the next century, we must insist on giving meaning to our repeated vow of "Never Again!" Because national courts will always be vulnerable to the threats and intimidation of murderous leaders, the world needs an international court that is beyond these tyrants' reach, a court that can serve as a backstop to local efforts to bring these killers to justice. If national efforts at justice fail, the world needs a tribunal capable of breaking the cycle of violence and impunity. Just as the Allies did in Nuremberg over 50 years ago, so today we must ensure that the pleas of victims are heard and that those who commit such crimes are brought to justice.

That is why I have asked the secretary of state, on behalf of the United States, to sign the treaty establishing an International Criminal Court. By signing the treaty, our nation manifests its profound commitment to subjecting the world's most heinous despots to the rule of law. We owe this commitment as a matter of justice to those who have suffered the depredations of the past. And we owe it to our children, because only by punishing today's mass murderers can we hope to deter the would-be killers of tomorrow. At the same time, I will begin active consultations with the Senate to prepare the way for early ratification, with the hope that the Senate's timely advice and consent will permit our nation to join this landmark institution as one of its 60 founding members.

I am proud to say that American support for the International Criminal Court is the latest step in a long tradition of American leadership in the fight to extend the rule of law and bring the world's worst criminals to justice. The United States was a central force behind the Nuremberg Tribunal, which prosecuted the authors of the Holocaust. U.S. leadership was key to establishing and supporting the International War Crimes Tribunal for the Former Yugoslavia, which has indicted many of the architects of

Other Council Policy Initiatives and Independent Task Force Reports Sponsored by the Council on Foreign Relations

* † *Future Visions for U.S. Defense Policy: Four Alternatives Presented as Presidential Speeches* (1998)—A Council Policy Initiative
John Hillen, Project Director

* † *Future Visions for U.S. Trade Policy* (1998)—A Council Policy Initiative
Bruce Stokes, Project Director

* † *Strengthening Palestinian Public Institutions* (1999)
Michael Rocard, Chair; Henry Siegman, Project Director

* † *U.S.-Cuban Relations in the 21st Century* (1999)
Bernard W. Aronson and William D. Rogers, Co-Chairs

* † *The Future of Transatlantic Relations* (1999)
Robert D. Blackwill, Chair and Project Director

* † *After the Tests: U.S. Policy Toward India and Pakistan* (1998)
Richard N. Haass and Morton H. Halperin, Co-Chairs; Cosponsored by the Brookings Institution

* † *Managing Change on the Korean Peninsula* (1998)
Morton I. Abramowitz and James T. Laney, Co-Chairs; Michael J. Green, Project Director

* † *Promoting U.S. Economic Relations with Africa* (1998)
Peggy Dulany and Frank Savage, Co-Chairs; Salih Booker, Project Manager

* † *Differentiated Containment: U.S. Policy Toward Iran and Iraq* (1997)
Zbigniew Brzezinski and Brent Scowcroft, Co-Chairs

† *Russia, Its Neighbors, and an Enlarging NATO* (1997)
Richard G. Lugar, Chair

* † *Financing America's Leadership: Protecting American Interests and Promoting American Values* (1997)
Mickey Edwards and Stephen J. Solarz, Co-Chairs

* *Rethinking International Drug Control: New Directions for U.S. Policy* (1997)
Mathea Falco, Chair

† *A New U.S. Policy Toward India and Pakistan* (1997)
Richard N. Haass, Chair; Gideon Rose, Project Director

* † *U.S. Middle East Policy and the Peace Process* (1997)
Henry Siegman, Project Coordinator

* *Arms Control and the U.S.-Russian Relationship: Problems, Prospects, and Prescriptions* (1996)
Robert D. Blackwill, Chair and Author; Keith W. Dayton, Project Director

† *American National Interests and the United Nations* (1996)
George Soros, Chair

---

*Available from Brookings Institution Press ($5.00 per copy). To order, call 1-800-275-1447.
†Available on the Council on Foreign Relations website at www.foreignrelations.org.

Toward an International Criminal Court?

Three Options

Presented as

Presidential Speeches

Alton Frye, Project Director

A Council Policy Initiative

Sponsored by the Council on Foreign Relations

The Council on Foreign Relations, Inc., a nonprofit, nonpartisan national membership organization founded in 1921, is dedicated to promoting understanding of international affairs through the free and civil exchange of ideas. The Council's members are dedicated to the belief that America's peace and prosperity are firmly linked to that of the world. From this flows the Council's mission: to foster America's understanding of other nations—their peoples, cultures, histories, hopes, quarrels, and ambitions—and thus to serve our nation through study and debate, private and public.

THE COUNCIL TAKES NO INSTITUTIONAL POSITION ON POLICY ISSUES AND HAS NO AFFILIATION WITH THE U.S. GOVERNMENT. ALL STATEMENTS OF FACT AND EXPRESSIONS OF OPINION CONTAINED IN ALL ITS PUBLICATIONS ARE THE SOLE RESPONSIBILITY OF THE AUTHOR OR AUTHORS.

This volume is the third in a series of Council Policy Initiatives (CPIs) designed to encourage debate among interested Americans on crucial foreign policy topics by presenting the issues and policy choices in terms easily understood by experts and nonexperts alike. The substance of the volume benefited from the comments of several analysts and many reviewers, but responsibility for the final text remains with the project director and the authors.

Other Council Policy Initiatives:

Future Visions for U.S. Defense Policy (1998), John Hillen, Project Director; *Future Visions for U.S. Trade Policy* (1998), Bruce Stokes, Project Director.

Council on Foreign Relations Books, Task Force Reports, and CPIs are distributed by Brookings Institution Press (1-800-275-1447). For further information on Council publications, please write the Council on Foreign Relations, 58 East 68th Street, New York, NY 10021, or call the Office of Communications at (212) 434-9400. Visit our website at www.foreignrelations.org.

Copyright © 1999 by the Council on Foreign Relations®, Inc.

All rights reserved.

Printed in the United States of America.

This book may not be reproduced, in whole or in part, in any form (beyond that copying permitted by Sections 107 and 108 of the U.S. Copyright Law and excerpts by reviewers for the public press), without written permission from the publisher. For information, write Publications Office, Council on Foreign Relations, 58 East 68th Street, New York, NY 10021.

CONTENTS

FOREWORD

Toward an International Criminal Court? is the third in a series of Council Policy Initiatives (CPIs) launched by the Council on Foreign Relations in 1997. The purpose of a CPI is to illuminate diverse approaches to key international issues on which a policy consensus is not readily achievable. By clarifying a range of relevant perspectives on such issues, the Council hopes to inform and enhance the public debate over choices facing American foreign policy.

In pursuing that objective, a CPI follows a straightforward process:

1. Having chosen a topic of significance and controversy, the Council enlists knowledgeable authors of divergent opinions to argue the case for the policy option each would recommend to a U.S. president.

2. Each option takes the form of a draft speech that a president might make in presenting a decision to the American people.

3. Panels of other experts subject those speeches to critical review, an unofficial evaluation process that resembles interagency deliberations within the government.

4. After thorough revision, the speeches are published under the cover of a memorandum arraying the options as a senior presidential adviser might do.

5. The published speeches and memorandum then serve as the basis for televised debates in New York or Washington and meetings around the country.

The Council takes no institutional position on any policy question but seeks to present the best case for each plausible option a president—and fellow citizens—would wish to consider.

The proposal for an International Criminal Court (ICC) has now advanced to a climactic stage requiring careful attention and serious thought. This study makes clear both the court's ambitious goals and the disputed factors bearing on American policy toward it. The Council is deeply grateful to the study's four principal authors: Anne-Marie Slaughter, Kenneth Roth, John Bolton, and Ruth Wedgwood. I would also like to thank Project Director Alton Frye for organizing the CPI and for bringing it to a successful conclusion. In supervising and integrating the study, Alton Frye has been ably supported by Hoyt Webb and by Research Associate Shane Smith.

I would like to express special gratitude to Arthur Ross and his foundation for not only supporting this project but also their general support of efforts by the Council to bring important issues to interested Americans in ways that non-experts can understand and debate.

The war crimes indictments of Yugoslav President Slobodan Milosevic and his senior associates, recently handed down by the ad hoc U.N. Tribunal for the Former Yugoslavia, make the subject of this CPI even more timely and compelling. As the U.S. policy community and interested citizens come to focus on the ICC's far-reaching implications, we trust that this CPI will contribute a useful measure of fact, logic, and hardheaded argument. In that task, it exemplifies the continuing mission of the Council on Foreign Relations.

Leslie H. Gelb
President

ACKNOWLEDGMENTS

The idea for this Council Policy Initiative originated with Morton Halperin, then a Council senior fellow and more recently director of policy planning in the Department of State. In addition to the authors, the Council wishes to thank those who gave the authors critical reviews, gentle nudges, and pointed suggestions. Participants in the panel reviews of the developing manuscripts included the following:

Project Director
and Editor: Alton Frye, *Council on Foreign Relations*

Panel
Reviewers: Elliot Abrams, *Ethics and Public Policy Center*
Lori Fisler Damrosch, *Columbia University*
Allan Gerson, *Council on Foreign Relations*
Wallace C. Gregson, *U.S. Marine Corps*
John Levitsky, *U.S. Department of State*
William Pace, *NGO Coalition for the International Criminal Court*
Michael Peters, *Council on Foreign Relations*
Daniel Bruce Poneman, *Hogan & Hartson*
John B. Rhinelander, *Shaw, Pittman, Potts & Trowbridge*
Barbara Paul Robinson, *Debevoise & Plimpton*
Frederick F. Roggero, *Council on Foreign Relations*
David Scheffer, *U.S. Department of State*
Jeffrey H. Smith, *Arnold & Porter*
Hoyt Webb, *Brown & Wood, LLP*

Research
  Associate and
  Rapporteur: Shane Smith, *Council on Foreign Relations*

By definition, the speeches and the cover memorandum stand as the individual work of the authors; none of the reviewers bears responsibility for any element of this volume. For their exceptional assistance in research and drafting the introductory memorandum, the project director and Professor Slaughter express their gratitude to Hoyt Webb and David Bosco.

Special appreciation goes to Director of Publications Patricia Dorff and her assistant, Miranda Kobritz, as well as to Council Vice President and Publisher David Kellogg, for their diligent professionalism in the editing and production of the finished work.

We also wish to express our warm thanks to the Arthur Ross Foundation, whose generous support made the project possible.

MEMORANDUM TO THE PRESIDENT

Anne-Marie Slaughter

FROM: "The National Security Adviser"

SUBJECT: Evaluating the International Criminal Court; Policy Speech Options

PURPOSE

In July 1998, after years of preparatory work and five weeks of negotiations in Rome, 120 states voted to approve a "statute," or treaty, establishing an International Criminal Court (ICC), with jurisdiction over genocide, crimes against humanity, war crimes, and the still-undefined crime of aggression. Despite our strong interest in creating a court, the United States voted against the Rome Statute, concluding that it could pose an unacceptable risk to U.S. military personnel and to your ability as commander in chief to deploy forces·worldwide to protect the United States and global interests. A year later, as our principal allies prepare to ratify the statute and bring the court into being, it is time to take a clear position supporting it, opposing it, or specifying the changes needed for our support.

The United States has actively supported the establishment of such a court since 1995. The immediate question is whether *this* court—the court negotiated in Rome—will be able to achieve enough of the benefits we seek from a permanent international court at an acceptable cost. Some now argue that, on balance, any such court would disserve American interests. Others contend that with the court becoming a reality, the costs of not joining far outweigh the costs of joining.

The conflict in Yugoslavia sharpens this debate and hastens the need for a decision. Although the actions of Yugoslav President Slobodan Milosevic and his subordinates fall under the jurisdiction of the ad hoc tribunal established by the United Nations to prosecute war crimes in the former Yugoslavia, the expulsion of hundreds of thousands of ethnic Albanians from Kosovo—and the massacre of many—is a chilling example of the kinds of crimes the ICC is intended to punish. Supporters of the court in its present form insist that only an effective permanent court can make the prospect of punishment for such atrocities sufficiently certain to deter their commission. Opponents of the ICC draw on the Kosovo crisis to bolster their claim that the court could be turned against us. They point out that when the Russian foreign minister initially denounced the NATO bombing campaign, he called for U.S. and other NATO leaders to be held accountable in accordance with international law. Indeed Milosevic himself asked the World Court to declare the bombing illegal, but the court found that it lacked jurisdiction (although it promised "fuller consideration" of the jurisdictional question at a later date). Independent of the merits of this debate, the apparent conflict between our humanitarian justification for NATO action and our vote against the ICC in July 1998 feeds suspicion and confusion about our foreign policy.

Beyond Kosovo, our position on the court will affect our ability to exercise leadership in shaping the international order for the next century. A historic trend in international law since 1945, accelerated since the end of the Cold War, has been to hold governments accountable for the treatment of their own citizens and to hold individual officials accountable for government actions. Thus, a critical challenge for the 21st century will be to develop institutions designed to regulate individuals as well as states within a global rule of law. The ICC debate gives us a chance to articulate a vision of what those institutions should look like—whether they should be national or international, permanent or ad hoc, global or regional. The result will be part of the legacy of your administration.

[2]

This memorandum reviews the development of international criminal law since 1945 and the evolution of U.S. policy toward an ICC. It provides a comparative analysis of three basic policies toward the ICC, followed by three draft speeches, each presenting and justifying a clearly articulated policy toward the proposed ICC.

Option One: Endorse the ICC—Sign as Is and Ratify When Possible

In spite of its current imperfections, the ICC established by the Rome Statute advances our interests and affirms our ideals. Tyrants guilty of mass atrocities against their own people and their neighbors threaten regional stability and ultimately global order, forcing us to impose sanctions and often to send soldiers. The ICC will serve notice on leaders like Milosevic and Saddam Hussein that they will be held responsible for their actions, thereby creating a meaningful deterrent. Equally important, it gives U.S. policymakers a standing mechanism for responding to horrific crimes committed against millions of victims, a response demanded by the American people and essential to the moral fabric of the nation. Regarding the danger that the ICC could be used against the United States, the Rome Statute provides more than adequate safeguards for American troops and leaders from frivolous prosecutions. In any event, with the court becoming a fait accompli, the best protection would be to sign and ratify the statute and thus ensure that U.S. involvement in the selection of judges and prosecutors will render this scenario almost impossible.

Option Two: Reject and Oppose the ICC

The current formulation of ICC jurisdiction in the Rome Statute contains serious defects that threaten U.S. freedom of action and expose America's civilian and military leaders and its servicemen and women to politically motivated prosecutions. The text adopted in Rome does not allow an adequate role for the U.N. Security Council, includes vague definitions of crimes that are susceptible to abuse, and exposes U.S. leaders and troops to a largely unaccountable prosecutor. Moreover, the prohibition on reservations to the statute is inconsistent with U.S. law and establishes a dangerous precedent. Perhaps most serious is the planned court's claim to exercise jurisdiction over even nonparties in certain situations. This encroachment on American constitutional safeguards requires that the United States not only reject the statute, but that it actively oppose the court.

Option Three: Improve the ICC—Cooperate as a Nonparty While Working for Changes

The broad goals of the ICC align with American interests in the promotion of international law and justice. The Rome Conference made much progress toward achieving a specific treaty text compatible with U.S. interests. The ICC project therefore deserves continuing American support and engagement. Yet serious deficiencies in the statute remain, deficiencies that must at least delay signature and ratification. These include the statute's undefined jurisdiction over aggression, inadequate limits on the initiation of prosecutions, and a last-minute provision related to Israel's policy toward settlements in occupied territories. Above all, the United States must strengthen guarantees that American military personnel will not be prosecuted internationally without U.S. concurrence. A stance of continued engagement, however, offers the best prospects for clarification of the court's mandate and confirms our dedication to human rights and justice.

A Possible Synthesis

While not developed in draft speech form, one can imagine synthesizing elements of Options One and Three. *There was some suspicion at Rome that the United States was urging changes in the text without committing itself to sign the agreement if they were accepted.* The U.S. delegation to the Preparatory Commission meetings could make clear that in exchange for key modifications to provide enhanced protection for American troops and policymakers, the United States will sign the statute. Specific reforms should include an "official acts" exception, assurances that Status of Forces Agreements (SOFAs) will immunize U.S. troops from foreign prosecution, and measures ensuring that nonparty countries cannot bring charges before the court without submitting to investigation themselves. We should work with our major allies to make their ratification and continued support for the court contingent on securing our signature. They are more likely to do so if we make clear that these proposed changes will elicit our signature rather than set the stage for further demands to alter the text negotiated in Rome.

Following this memorandum are the three basic options presented as speeches so that you can get a feel for how each case could be made. Each speech varies in form as well as content; each takes a very strong position in favor of one of the options. The hope is to clarify the issues and their implications in order to help you formulate your own position.

The ICC stands at the crossroads of American grand strategy, the search for global justice, and the changing architecture of the international system. Moreover, the decision concerning the ICC arises at the end of a decade of post–Cold War disorder resulting from ethnic and religious conflicts, failed states, civil wars, and local and regional power struggles. The crisis in Kosovo highlights fundamental questions regarding not only lessons learned from previous conflicts but also changing views about the design of global and regional security regimes. The discussion that follows does not address these larger concerns; it can only indicate how a particular position on the ICC might intersect with them.

BACKGROUND

After World War II, the international community, outraged at the atrocities committed by the Nazi regime, took action at Nuremberg against many of the leaders responsible. The Nuremberg trials, in turn, helped establish a basic framework and precedent for the prosecution of war crimes and crimes against humanity. The Geneva Conventions of 1949 codified and expanded the rules of war and included basic protections for civilians and combatants involved in civil war. The International Law Commission formulated the Nuremberg Principles in 1950 and concluded a draft Code of

Offenses against the Peace and Security of Mankind in 1954. But the development of a regime holding individuals accountable for crimes under international law slowed considerably during the Cold War.

The chronology of crimes since Nuremberg is long. In Cambodia, the Khmer Rouge was responsible for approximately two million deaths and disappearances during its bloody rule in the 1970s. In El Salvador, government troops bent on subduing an insurgency attacked and killed civilians, including children, as they hunted their enemy. A strong case can be made that Iraq's Saddam Hussein committed genocide by ordering the chemical weapons attack on Kurdish villages in northern Iraq and that his gruesome treatment of Kuwaiti prisoners during the Gulf War constituted war crimes. At least half a million people were killed and others maimed in the Rwandan genocide in 1994. From 1992 to 1995, Bosnian Serb forces engaged in a massive ethnic cleansing campaign affecting several hundred thousand people and culminating in the massacre of more than seven thousand men at Srebrenica. And 1999 saw the displacement of a million or more Kosovars, along with numerous murders, rapes, and other acts of ethnic brutality.

In the face of these tragedies, the United States has led efforts to achieve some measure of justice. We have been the leading supporter of the War Crimes Tribunals established by the United Nations for the former Yugoslavia and for Rwanda. We have provided funds, attorneys, investigators, and other staff, including military and intelligence assistance for their operations. With U.S. support, both tribunals have made significant progress. The International Criminal Tribunal for the Former Yugoslavia has in its custody almost one-third of the individuals publicly indicted and has passed down several sentences. NATO forces in Bosnia recently arrested a general alleged to be responsible for operations at Srebrenica. Moreover, the existence of the tribunal has contributed to isolating extremist elements in Bosnia and discouraged their resistance to the NATO-led peacekeeping effort there. The War Crimes Tribunal for Rwanda has in custody several key organizers of the 1994 genocide and recently handed down precedent-setting convictions for genocide. The United States is currently promoting the establishment of an international tribunal to prosecute leaders of the Khmer Rouge.

The ICC itself has been a long time in the making. The United Nations envisioned such a court soon after Nuremberg, but the project foundered during the Cold War. The tribunals for the former Yugoslavia and for Rwanda breathed new life into the project and taught the international community valuable lessons about international criminal prosecution. Importantly, the tribunals helped further develop the international law that could be applied by the ICC. But the process of creating and operating the individual tribunals has been expensive and redundant, providing an additional reason for the creation of a standing ICC.

In the presidential address to the U.N. General Assembly in September 1997 the United States called for the establishment of a permanent international court to prosecute the most serious violations of international humanitarian law. The U.S. ambassador for war crimes (a position created in 1997) led the U.S. delegation to the Rome Conference and played a major role in laying the groundwork for the ICC. Congressional support for a court, however, has been considerably more muted. Leading internationalists in Congress were almost entirely silent on the issue during the Rome Conference. Shortly before the conference, the Pentagon took the unusual step of calling together allied military attachés to discuss the statute. It opposes such elements as the lack of Security Council control of prosecutions, the inclusion of aggression as a crime, and the scope of some of the war crimes provisions.

Over the course of five weeks of complex negotiations in Rome, the United States found itself in opposition to a large group led by some of our closest allies, including Germany, Canada, and Britain, all of whom strongly support a court. The American delegation achieved some very significant successes in protecting U.S. interests during the drafting process but was ultimately unable to support the final text of the Rome Statute. The final vote on the statute was 120 to 7; voting with the United States in opposition were Iraq, Libya, Qatar, Yemen, China, and Israel. The Rome Statute will come into effect when 60 nations have signed and ratified it; at present, 82 nations have signed, and 3 have ratified, though many more are making preparations to do so. In particular, the French, German, British, and Italian governments are all taking the preliminary steps necessary to ratify.

A detailed list of U.S. objections to the statute, drawn from Ambassador David Scheffer's statement before the Senate Foreign Relations Committee on July 23, 1998, is reprinted in Appendix A. Public debate since the conclusion of the Rome Conference has focused on four key concerns:

- The danger that U.S. military personnel could be brought before the ICC for political reasons.

- The degree of Security Council control over prosecutions initiated by the ICC prosecutor.

- The ambiguity of the crimes over which the ICC would exercise jurisdiction, particularly the crime of aggression, which could conceivably extend to some U.S. troop deployments, and the alleged crime of settlement in an occupied territory, which would arguably implicate Israeli leaders for activities in the West Bank and the Gaza Strip.

- The relationship between the ICC and national judicial processes.

Since the conclusion of the Rome Conference, the United States has been actively participating in Preparatory Commission meetings designed to reach agreement on outstanding issues necessary to make the court fully operational.

THE OPTIONS

As you read the distilled options below and the draft speeches that follow, it is important for you to bear in mind one general caveat and two specific points. Arguments for the different options mix moral, political, and pragmatic concerns in ways that frequently lead proponents of different positions to speak past each other.

At a philosophical level, the debate focuses on the moral obligations of the United States. Option One contends that the United States must do all it can to prevent mass atrocities when it can do so at reasonable cost. In Option Two, the moral imperative animating the court is balanced against and ultimately outweighed by the imperative of protecting American liberties, sovereignty, and constitutional processes from any encroachment.

In part, this debate hinges on the anticipated functioning of the ICC: Will it be used responsibly or irresponsibly? But the positions also reflect very different attitudes toward the development and expansion of international law. Option One presents international law as a firm ally of American interests and a consistent goal of American policy, while in Option Two it is treated as an increasing danger to American liberties and effective foreign policy. At the heart of this debate is the unavoidable question of how much sovereignty the United States is willing to sacrifice to aid in the fortification of a global rule of law.

At a policy level, the options differ on the likely effects of the ICC. Option One presents the court as an institution that will further peace and security while eventually limiting the need for costly and dangerous foreign deployments. This forecast rests on two assumptions. The first is that holding particular individuals responsible to the international community for their crimes will break self-perpetuating cycles of violence and impunity. The second is that prosecutions will have a deterrent effect on would-be perpetrators. Option Two is much more dubious about the ability of the court to promote peace and security effectively because it questions both whether peace and justice are always compatible and whether the ICC will have any meaningful deterrent effect. Option Three accepts the main premises of Option One but concedes that some of the concerns raised in Option Two require additional safeguards to those provided in the Rome text.

At a pragmatic level, the debate is about simple institutional efficiency. Both Options One and Three make the case that the ICC is a better long-term solution than continued ad hoc tribunals, each of which must begin largely from scratch and is subject to veto in the U.N. Security Council. Moreover, as a single, ongoing structure the ICC would avoid problems of inconsistent judgments that can arise with separate, ad hoc structures. (It was to ameliorate this problem that the Rwandan and Yugoslav tribunals share a prosecutor's office and appeals chamber.) In Option Two, however, the gains in institutional efficiency matter very little when weighed against the dangers to American freedom of action and sovereignty.

More specifically, you should keep in mind the following premises underlying all the options:

- The options presented here often discuss the advantages and disadvantages of the ICC in the context of U.S. signature and approval by the Senate. Yet most observers agree that even with a full-scale administration effort, ratification is highly unlikely in the present political context. This memorandum lists the likely consequences of an effort to secure ratification, if you decide to submit the statute to the Senate. However, even without ratification, signature would impose an obligation under international law not to undercut the provisions of the statute pending the Senate's decision on whether or not to tender its advice and consent.

- The options presented assume that the basic structure of the Rome Statute will remain unaltered. But as noted above, the United States has been participating in Preparatory Commission work since the completion of the conference and will attempt to introduce certain changes before the final treaty enters into force; the fate of these proposals is uncertain.

A brief explanation of the strengths, weaknesses, and political impact of each option follows.

OPTION ONE: ENDORSE THE ICC—SIGN AS IS AND
RATIFY WHEN POSSIBLE

Summary
The ICC established by the Rome Statute is a cost-effective institution for addressing the most serious violations of human-

itarian law, human rights law, and the law of war. It will avoid the recurring need to expend energy and political capital to establish ad hoc tribunals to investigate crimes committed in particular countries or conflicts. Equally important, as a permanent mechanism its deterrent effect is likely to be far greater. To the extent it succeeds as a deterrent, the court will reduce the necessity of costly and dangerous deployments. Even absent any deterrent effect, however, it will advance core U.S. values, including respect for the rule of law, due process, and individual accountability. It will also strengthen relations with key allies and make it easier for us to exercise leadership through existing multilateral institutions.

These benefits far outweigh any potential costs imposed on the United States. The Rome Statute provides more than adequate safeguards for American troops and leaders from frivolous prosecutions; moreover, the active involvement of the United States in the selection of judges and prosecutors will render such scenarios almost impossible.

Therefore, the administration should sign the statute as soon as possible and seek Senate advice and consent when that becomes feasible. The United States should not seek to reopen negotiations on the statute. Even without ratification, a U.S. signature will signal commitment to the court and help ensure that American influence will be felt at every stage of the court's development.

Strengths
- Ensures that the United States will enjoy full voting rights in the appointment of prosecutors and judges and in establishing working procedures for the ICC.

- Enhances the likelihood that the ICC will become an effective and relevant institution.

- Strengthens relations with our allies and reestablishes U.S. leadership in the development of international institutions.

- Affirms fundamental U.S. values as a force for human rights and the rule of law.

Weaknesses

- Reverses the course set in Rome last summer and accepts a statute we have denounced as insufficient to protect U.S. troops from prosecution before a non-U.S. judicial body.

- Forfeits leverage to seek any future changes in the statute, both for us and for Israel.

- Lacks support in the Senate, setting up a costly and potentially distracting political battle.

Political Impact

- In the Senate, you are likely to face strong opposition on both sides of the aisle. Many senators are very concerned about the potential prosecution not only of U.S. troops but of Israeli leaders for their actions in the occupied territories; others would prefer to spend their energy on other important international issues.

- In Congress, opposition to the court would likely continue even after a successful ratification bid through efforts to block funding for the court and resistance to foreign deployments of American forces without an absolute guarantee against prosecution arising from such operations.

- In the Pentagon, all the services will be strongly opposed on the grounds that the existence of an ICC with any possibility of prosecuting U.S. servicemen and women will hamper military decision-making at headquarters and in the field. Ratification of the statute may provide opponents of peacekeeping and humanitarian assistance operations with additional ammunition.

- Among the general public, you will have to mount a major campaign to educate voters about the court and counter charges that it infringes our sovereignty. But a public debate about the court could offer a valuable opportunity to strengthen support for your foreign policy goals.

- Among allies, a decision to sign and even to seek ratification will have strong support; such a decision may also strengthen support for the United States in the international community generally. The prominent exception will be Israel, which will remain opposed and feel isolated without the United States.

OPTION TWO: REJECT AND OPPOSE THE ICC

Summary

The Rome Statute is seriously flawed and would establish a court that would be contrary to the national interests and the constitutional experience of the United States. As a matter of domestic law, the Rome Statute could not be ratified on a "take it or leave it" basis without violating the Senate's constitutional prerogative to attach reservations. Absent such reservations, American political and military leaders would face the prospect of politically motivated prosecutions before a judicial organ beyond the reach of the U.S. Constitution. Moreover, the ICC prosecutor is empowered beyond the bounds of normal U.S. prosecutors, and the jurisdiction of the court is overbroad, reaching to nonparties in some circumstances. Certain crimes are also defined in relatively vague terms, leaving them susceptible to prosecutorial abuse.

In light of these defects, the United States must not only refuse to sign the Rome Statute, it must actively oppose the ICC. Specifically, the United States should pursue a policy of "three noes": The United States should provide no financial support for the court, directly or indirectly; the administration should not collaborate further in efforts to make the court operational; and the United States should not negotiate further with governments to "improve" the ICC. This policy will maximize the chances that the court will not come into existence.

Strengths

- Avoids an international commitment that arguably could conflict with constitutional due process protections and that many see as a fundamental challenge to American sovereignty.

- Bolsters the U.S. position that the Rome Statute cannot apply to nonparty states should the ICC undertake an investigation hostile to American interests.

- Avoids a confrontation with Senate opponents whose support is needed on other administration initiatives.

- Helps allay concerns that U.S. servicemen and women and leaders may be subject to prosecution, particularly if U.S. opposition prevents the court from functioning effectively. Reducing the alleged threat to U.S. military personnel would also reduce Pentagon objections to foreign deployments considered necessary by the administration.

- Signals U.S. commitment to maintaining the power of its Security Council veto in the establishment of international judicial bodies.

Weaknesses
- Reverses a policy of four years standing that has lent active support to the idea of a permanent international criminal court.

- Isolates the United States from key allies and diminishes U.S. credibility on human rights and humanitarian issues in the broader international community.

- Overlooks U.S. participation in numerous treaties that permit U.S. citizens to be held accountable for criminal and even economic actions in foreign jurisdictions.

- Prevents the United States from making use of ICC machinery to pursue indictments against future perpetrators of atrocities, forcing reliance on further ad hoc measures unlikely to be supported by allies.

Political Impact
- In Congress, unilateralists will enthusiastically endorse this approach but could use it as a platform to oppose a wide range of multilateral initiatives and institutions supported by the

administration. Others who would not necessarily support ratification are likely nevertheless to question open opposition to the court.

- In the Pentagon, reactions are likely to range from mild to strong support, although some military leaders will prefer to support a more circumscribed court, especially if it were constrained to act only on the Security Council's recommendation.

- In the broader public, a reversal of policy and active opposition to the court could strengthen forces opposed to the United Nations and other international organizations, although absent a ratification debate the public salience of the issue will remain low.

- Among national human rights organizations and other groups, this option will spark anger and mobilization against the administration.

- Among our allies, a decision definitively to reject the statute will harden the perception of U.S. exceptionalism and hostility to the development of universally applicable international law. Moreover, rejecting the court will put U.S. policy in direct conflict with close allies whose cooperation is necessary for a host of policy goals.

OPTION THREE: IMPROVE THE ICC—COOPERATE
AS A NONPARTY

Summary
The Rome negotiations were on the right track, but they ended prematurely and failed to include adequate safeguards for U.S. troops and other protections that would take account of the unique role of the U.S. military in conducting global operations. Nevertheless, the ICC's mandate over genocide, war crimes, and crimes against humanity serves the broad U.S. interest of promoting the rule of law and global justice. We thus have a continuing interest in

working to improve and clarify the text of the Rome Statute and in supporting humanitarian, peacekeeping, and other missions necessitated by actions that will fall within the court's jurisdiction.

As the ICC structure and rules develop, the administration should seek greater protection for American troops deployed abroad and for U.S. political leaders. Without requiring any change in treaty language, the administration can seek binding interpretations of the existing text in the Rome Preparatory Commission to preserve America's necessary latitude in making military decisions.

The Preparatory Commission should provide clear, binding interpretations that the ICC will respect military judgments unless they are "manifestly unlawful" and will never require the presentation of classified information to justify controversial targeting decisions. Similarly, binding interpretive statements should make clear that the court will honor U.S. Status of Forces Agreements, for these protect American troops serving abroad from arrest by host countries. In addition, the crime of aggression should remain outside the ICC's jurisdiction for any state that has not endorsed the court's definition and for nonstate parties, at least in cases not referred by the Security Council.

Strengths
- Demonstrates U.S. commitment to the broad goals of the ICC while maintaining our freedom of action if the sought-after changes are not adopted. Meanwhile, a nonconfrontational stance will maximize the chance for adoption of these changes.

- Delays a difficult ratification battle while waiting for the court to prove itself (in the short term) by the quality of its appointments and (in the medium to long term) by effectively carrying out investigations and indictments. Also gives time to generate broader support for the court both in the Senate and among the American people.

- Maintains a degree of cohesion with key allies on this issue and avoids a needless schism within NATO.

Weaknesses
- Forfeits a strong U.S. leadership role in the establishment of a new generation of international institutions. Reduces U.S. influence in the staffing and direction of the court.

- Risks the possibility of another embarrassing rejection of U.S. proposals after another round of negotiation in which the administration is visibly engaged. Such rejection would only harden American sentiment against multilateral engagement.

- Invites criticism of the administration as indecisive, capable only of adopting a wait-and-see approach.

Political Impact
- In the Senate, opponents of the ICC are likely to denounce this position as the worst of both worlds—the United States is not a party and does not have a vote for judges and prosecutors, yet its cooperation gives the court legitimacy that it would not have otherwise.

- The Pentagon may well support this strategy if the administration makes clear its commitment to near-absolute guarantees against international prosecution of American troops without U.S. consent.

- In the broader public, this option is unlikely to have any significant impact. Human rights groups should see it as a major improvement over Option Two.

- With allies, a policy of cooperation will certainly be more welcome than outright rejection. By working closely with allies who have signed the statute, the United States could likely have significant impact on the development of rules and the further definition of crimes. Still, the negotiating process that this approach will entail may lead to a recurrence of the friction witnessed in the 1998 Rome Conference.

RECOMMENDATION

Convene your senior national security advisers informally to review this memo in the expectation that the court will come into being.

1. Identify specific guidelines for our delegation to the Preparatory Commission negotiations.

2. Prepare to adopt a revised position on the ICC before your forthcoming address to the U.N. General Assembly.

The position adopted should take into account both continuing efforts by signatories to the ICC statute to shape the court and the immediate context of our efforts to establish peace and justice in the Balkans. Joining the court means accepting the same treaty obligations as the majority of U.S. allies and other states in the interest of creating an effective permanent institution to deal with the most heinous international crimes; not joining means giving priority to less constrained national decision-making while relying on ad hoc tribunals and other mechanisms to cope with such crimes.

SPEECH ONE: ENDORSE THE INTERNATIONAL CRIMINAL COURT

Kenneth Roth

My fellow Americans:

It is a sad fact that the twentieth century will be remembered as much for the unprecedented scale of its bloodshed and slaughter as for the remarkable progress made in technology, health, economic development, and the spread of democracy. The Holocaust; genocide in Rwanda, Bosnia, and Iraq; the depredations of Saddam Hussein, Idi Amin, Slobodan Milosevic, Pol Pot, and a host of other despots and murderers—too many lives have been lost, too many families broken, too many hopes and dreams snuffed out by this inhumanity.

If we are to eradicate this plague in the next century, we must insist at the very least that those responsible for such barbarity be arrested, tried, and punished. Half a century after America helped launch a system of international justice at Nuremberg, I stand with our democratic partners from around the world to reaffirm America's commitment to justice and the rule of law by embracing the new International Criminal Court.

The cause of this century's brutality is not simply the evil that lies in some men's hearts. It is also our collective failure to build on the Nuremberg precedent by ensuring that all such killers are brought to justice. Too often since the Holocaust, the cries of victims have gone unanswered. The pleas of survivors fell on unresponsive ears. The signal was sent to would-be murderers that there is no price to be paid for such horrendous crimes. This failure of justice bred further slaughter, in a vicious cycle of impunity and violence.

Saddam Hussein illustrates this dangerous cycle. In 1988, when he dropped chemical weapons on the people of the Iraqi city of Halabja, he became the only tyrant known to have directed these inhumane weapons against his own citizens. But no calls went out for his arrest. No indictments were issued. No tribunal was established for his prosecution.

Over the next six months, he repeatedly used chemical weapons against Iraq's Kurdish people, driving them from their homes and into the murderous hands of his security forces. One hundred thousand Kurdish men, women, and children were trucked to remote sites, lined up, and executed, their bodies bulldozed into unmarked graves.

Once more, Saddam Hussein was not brought to justice for this genocide. He was never made to pay a price for his crimes. This lesson emboldened him to invade Kuwait just two years later, with the resulting destruction and suffering that we all know too well.

A similar tale can be found in Cambodia. From 1975 to 1979, the Khmer Rouge inflicted a calamitous plague on the Cambodian people. Cities were emptied. Families were divided. People were murdered for as little as being educated or wearing glasses. Cambodian society was forcibly turned back to a pre-industrial age. As many as two million Cambodians lost their lives. Yet no one was prosecuted for these crimes against humanity. Pol Pot, the Khmer Rouge leader, lived for many years on the Thai-Cambodian border before dying a year ago. Other Khmer Rouge leaders, such as Ieng Sary, Khieu Samphan, and Noun Chea, have been welcomed back into Cambodian society, their crimes buried. Because of this failure of justice, political violence mars Cambodia's recovery to this day.

Too many others responsible for the atrocities of this century continue to enjoy impunity. From the Guatemalan military, for its scorched-earth slaughter of its native Indian population, to the Burundian government, for its massacre of ethnic Hutus, impunity has been the norm, prosecution the exception.

It is a sad irony that today a squeegee man on the streets of New York City stands a better chance of arrest, trial, and punishment than a genocidal killer. Far too often we have sent tyrants the message that they can escape justice if only their victims are sufficiently numerous, their reign sufficiently ruthless, their crimes sufficiently brutal.

It is not difficult to see why these mass murderers regularly escape justice. In many countries, prosecutors and judges enjoy no independence. A late-night phone call or an intimidating visit is frequently all it takes to discourage investigation or prosecution of official crimes. As added insurance, many tyrants decree amnesties for themselves to make it legally difficult to pursue their crimes.

As we look to the next century, we must insist on giving meaning to our repeated vow of "Never Again!" Because national courts will always be vulnerable to the threats and intimidation of murderous leaders, the world needs an international court that is beyond these tyrants' reach, a court that can serve as a backstop to local efforts to bring these killers to justice. If national efforts at justice fail, the world needs a tribunal capable of breaking the cycle of violence and impunity. Just as the Allies did in Nuremberg over 50 years ago, so today we must ensure that the pleas of victims are heard and that those who commit such crimes are brought to justice.

That is why I have asked the secretary of state, on behalf of the United States, to sign the treaty establishing an International Criminal Court. By signing the treaty, our nation manifests its profound commitment to subjecting the world's most heinous despots to the rule of law. We owe this commitment as a matter of justice to those who have suffered the depredations of the past. And we owe it to our children, because only by punishing today's mass murderers can we hope to deter the would-be killers of tomorrow. At the same time, I will begin active consultations with the Senate to prepare the way for early ratification, with the hope that the Senate's timely advice and consent will permit our nation to join this landmark institution as one of its 60 founding members.

I am proud to say that American support for the International Criminal Court is the latest step in a long tradition of American leadership in the fight to extend the rule of law and bring the world's worst criminals to justice. The United States was a central force behind the Nuremberg Tribunal, which prosecuted the authors of the Holocaust. U.S. leadership was key to establishing and supporting the International War Crimes Tribunal for the Former Yugoslavia, which has indicted many of the architects of "ethnic cleansing" in Bosnia and Kosovo. The United States played a similar role in helping to establish the War Crimes Tribunal for Rwanda, which has indicted and secured the custody of most of the leadership behind the Rwandan genocide. Both the Yugoslav and Rwandan tribunals are well along in the process of trying and convicting these killers. U.S. diplomats today are also working to establish parallel tribunals to address Saddam Hussein's crimes and the atrocities of the Khmer Rouge.

However, we must recognize the limits of this country-by-country approach to international justice. It is expensive and time-consuming to build each new country-specific tribunal from scratch. Moreover, in Iraq, Cambodia, and other sites of unthinkable atrocities, it has been impossible to secure the unanimous agreement among the five permanent members of the U.N. Security Council needed to authorize new, country-specific tribunals. Tyrants in these places are left to savor the fruits of their cruel and bloody reigns untroubled by the prospect of justice.

The International Criminal Court was born of a determination to move beyond the inadequacies of this country-by-country approach. In 1998 the nations of the world gathered in Rome to create a tribunal with global scope, one that would be available to prosecute and punish the world's worst offenders wherever they committed their crimes. The goal was to signal to tomorrow's would-be tyrants that there will be no more escaping justice, no more safe havens—that the international community will pursue these killers and prosecute them wherever they hide.

The Rome negotiators rightfully limited their focus to the gravest crimes—genocide, war crimes, and crimes against humanity. These crimes embrace such atrocities as systematic ethnic and political slaughter, widespread torture and rape, and the indiscriminate use of military force against civilians. In the name of the international community, the negotiators resolved that those who commit these unspeakable crimes must be brought to justice, that they must be prevented from using violence and intimidation to secure their impunity.

The Rome negotiations were difficult and complex. Negotiators had to merge different legal systems and different visions of the role of international justice. Although the U.S. delegation in Rome played a large role in shaping the court and defining its reach, focus, and powers, the delegation did not obtain everything it asked for. For that reason, while virtually all of our closest allies were celebrating the new court, our delegation reluctantly voted against it, making the United States one of only seven governments to oppose the court against 120 voting in favor of it.

Because the United States stood so isolated, I authorized an interagency review to reevaluate our position. Today, I am pleased to announce that this evaluative process has been completed and that the United States is ready to embrace this landmark institution for eradicating some of the worst horrors of our time. By signing the court's treaty and seeking its ratification, I hope that the United States will be among the court's founding members. But even if the Senate does not heed my call for prompt ratification, America's signing of the treaty represents a pledge of support for the court and its efforts to bring the world's most vicious tyrants to justice. It thus ensures that American experience and values continue to shape this historic institution and help it live up to the high ideals that guided the Rome deliberations.

In announcing American support for the court, I am proud to join not only with all of our closest NATO allies—including Canada, Britain, France, Germany, and Italy—but also with newly democratic governments around the world, such as Nelson Mandela's South Africa, Carlos Menem's Argentina, and Kim Dae Jung's South Korea. These new democracies, having recently escaped from authoritarian rule, understand perhaps even better than we do the importance of international justice to guard against renewed tyranny.

But the International Criminal Court is in the interest not only of America's allies. It is also in America's own interest. The inhuman crimes that are the focus of the court endanger the lawful and orderly world on which American peace and prosperity depend. On this increasingly interdependent globe, the aggression and turmoil that usually accompany severe abuses threaten our commerce, welfare, and even the security of our borders. Enhancing the rule of law to address these threats serves all Americans.

By contrast, doing nothing in the face of atrocities imperils our ideals. Sure as the beacon that shines from the Statue of Liberty, the world looks to the United States to uphold democracy, human rights, and the rule of law. America stands strong when we defend these ideals. But unanswered atrocities undermine the values on which our great nation was founded. America needs an International Criminal Court because we depend on the vision of humanity and the values of justice and law that it will defend. The court will uphold our belief that criminals should be held responsible for their actions and that victims should see their attackers brought to account.

The International Criminal Court is also in America's interest because it can help save the lives of our soldiers. In recent years, the most common reason for deploying American troops overseas has been to stop precisely the kind of slaughter and bloodshed that the court is designed to prevent. When genocide strikes, when crimes against humanity spread, when war crimes are committed, the United States, as the world's most powerful nation, has rightfully felt a duty to do what it can to stop the killing. Knowing the danger of these missions, knowing the risks that our brave young soldiers must run, we nonetheless have resolved as a nation to stand with victims against their tormentors. By helping to deter tomorrow's tyrants, the International Criminal Court will reduce the necessity of deploying American soldiers to stop their slaughter. That will mean fewer dangerous assignments for our armed forces and fewer young American lives at risk.

Of course, no court can be a perfect deterrent. Even America's own courts and law enforcement officials cannot dissuade every would-be criminal from a life outside the law. But the International Criminal Court offers great promise as a deterrent because it targets not an entire people, the way broad trade sanctions do; not frontline conscripts, the way military intervention often does; but the tyrant who is ordering and directing the killing. Some tyrants might still not be deterred. But even if the court prevents only an occasional genocide, it is worth it. Even if it avoids the need to deploy American troops on dangerous assignment overseas only sometimes, we have a duty to support it. For the benefit of humankind, for the security of our nation, and for the safety of our troops, we should join this historic institution.

To be sure, the International Criminal Court, like any court, will depend on governments to arrest suspects and enforce judgments. And governments sometimes hesitate to expose their troops to the dangers involved. Still, the international record so far has been encouraging. Most of the suspects indicted by the War Crimes Tribunal for Rwanda are now in custody, thanks largely to the efforts of many African nations. Our brave troops in Bosnia, joined by our NATO partners, have played a critical role in ensuring that those indicted by the Yugoslav tribunal are gradually brought to justice, although certain key leaders remain at large. But even if a suspect is never arrested, an indictment by the International Criminal Court will make the defendant a pariah for life, unable to travel abroad for fear of arrest and always worried that shifts in national politics might suddenly make it convenient for his government to surrender him. That fate itself could help deter would-be killers. And if deterrence fails, an indictment can help, at the very least, to mobilize popular support to fight tyranny. Slobodan Milosevic should not sleep well.

Like any new institution, the court generates fears among those who cannot yet know how it will operate. These apprehensions are understandable. But I have thought long and hard about these concerns and have concluded that the court in fact advances American interests, that we should not let these fears diminish our support for an institution that will extend the rule of law to those most in need. Let me explain why.

Perhaps the most common fear is that our enemies will use the court to launch frivolous or politically motivated charges against American soldiers or commanders. What if a renegade government wanted to embarrass the United States by asking the court to pursue a groundless prosecution of Americans? In my view, there are more than adequate safeguards against this contingency.

It is important to note at the outset that it is not the policy of the United States, nor do I believe it ever will become the policy of the United States, to commit genocide, war crimes, or crimes against humanity. These unspeakable acts are appropriately considered beyond the realm of civilized conduct. America should not fear the prosecution of these crimes because we as a nation do not commit them. Indeed, if a rogue American soldier were to violate orders and commit a war crime, it is our policy to prosecute that soldier vigorously ourselves. The academic debate about whether U.S. military conduct in the past might today be deemed criminal is irrelevant because the International Criminal Court will address only future conduct, and our future does not include committing these atrocities.

We oppose these crimes not only out of humanitarian concern for others but also because in doing so we protect ourselves and our own soldiers. For example, international law prohibiting war crimes helps protect American soldiers who might be captured from facing torture or execution. It helps defend against attacks on hospitals or ambulances that are treating our battlefield wounded. It helps protect our soldiers against attacks with such cruel and inhumane devices as chemical and biological weapons.

Some fear that the prohibitions of genocide, war crimes, and crimes against humanity are vague or elastic concepts that might be stretched to reach legitimate American military conduct. They are wrong. The crime of genocide is carefully defined by a treaty that the United States and 128 other nations have ratified. It addresses murder and other serious acts of violence committed with the intent to destroy all or part of a national, ethnic, racial, or religious group. Crimes against humanity were first brought to court with American assistance over 50 years ago at the Nuremberg Tribunal. They address widespread or systematic patterns of atrocities, including torture and rape. Most of the war crimes under the court's jurisdiction are defined in extensive detail by the Geneva Conventions, which the United States and 187 other nations have ratified, and their protocols, which the United States has signed and 152 states have ratified. They include many specific provisions designed to spare civilians the hazards of war. All of the conduct to be addressed by the court is already prohibited by the Pentagon's own military manuals. American forces do not commit these crimes, and it is in America's interest that others refrain from committing them as well.

There was one war crime that was of particular concern to those with reservations about the International Criminal Court—the crime prohibiting attacks on military targets that cause disproportionate harm to civilians. Again, it is not U.S. policy to engage in such attacks. But some feared that an American attack on a military target that inadvertently caused harm to civilians might inappropriately be found criminal. As a result, the court's treaty was drafted in language suggested by the U.S. delegation to make clear that this crime will be prosecuted only in the clearest of cases, not in the event of error or a second-guessed judgment call.

But imagine the remote possibility that an American soldier did commit a war crime. What if a soldier ran amok and executed prisoners or deliberately attacked civilians? Would that soldier face trial before the International Criminal Court? No. That is because, under the principle of "complementarity" codified in its treaty, the court will assume jurisdiction only when national courts are unwilling or unable to investigate and, if appropriate, prosecute the matter themselves. The International Criminal Court will not routinely substitute itself for national courts, where justice is most meaningful, but will encourage national courts to do the job themselves. Only when national court systems have broken down, or abusive governments insist on shielding criminal suspects from legitimate investigation and prosecution, will the International Criminal Court step in. Indeed, the court must defer to good faith investigation by national law enforcement personnel whether or not they conclude that the evidence warrants prosecution. Because, as I have noted, it is firm American policy to prosecute any rogue soldier who might commit a war crime, there will be no need for an American suspect ever to be brought before the court.

To avoid any possibility of the International Criminal Court reviewing legitimate military judgments, some critics have suggested that the court's statute be amended to allow governments to exempt their soldiers' conduct by declaring it to have been officially authorized. Because the United States would not declare any genuinely abusive conduct to be official policy, the thinking goes, such a rule would keep the court focused on the most heinous crimes, not borderline cases. Unfortunately, other governments would not be so reticent. No less a crime than the Holocaust was the product of official Nazi policy. Because governments at times do commit atrocities deliberately, conduct should not be exempted just because it was officially sanctioned.

Some have asked whether we can trust the judges of a future International Criminal Court to apply the court's rules fairly. Will they defer to American investigations and prosecutions, as the court's treaty requires? How will we ensure that the court does not become a politicized tool that might hound Americans?

The answer is that the International Criminal Court is not a political body, such as the United Nations, or even a tribunal to resolve political disputes between states, such as the International Court of Justice, the so-called World Court. Instead, the International Criminal Court will have the fact-specific task of determining whether evidence exists to investigate or prosecute a particular suspect for a specific crime. The history of other international criminal tribunals gives us strong reason to have confidence in such a court.

For example, the chief prosecutors of the Yugoslav and Rwandan War Crimes Tribunals have exemplified the integrity and professionalism needed to conduct such sensitive criminal inquiries. The first chief prosecutor, Justice Richard Goldstone of South Africa, brought with him the dedication to the rule of law that he showed as the jurist who exposed the apartheid government's role in fomenting violence. Today he is a member of post-apartheid South Africa's new Constitutional Court.

His successor, Judge Louise Arbour, had an equally impressive career as a judge and defender of individual rights in Canada. Both are highly respected jurists who as chief war crimes prosecutors paid scrupulous attention to due process and the rights of the accused. Similarly, the tribunals' chief judge is America's own Gabrielle Kirk McDonald, a distinguished federal district court judge from Texas who has had a long career fighting racial discrimination and upholding the rule of law in the United States. The conduct of these jurists and their colleagues on the War Crimes Tribunals has been exemplary.

There is every reason to believe that the leadership of the International Criminal Court will show similar professionalism. The judges and prosecutor will be chosen by the governments that join the court, including most of our closest allies. Indeed, because joining the court means subjecting oneself to its jurisdiction, the court's membership is likely to be tilted in favor of the world's democracies, which will have a strong interest in the court's integrity. Moreover, because the court will be established with or without us, the best way to ensure its professionalism is for the United States to join our allies and play a prominent role in selecting its judges and prosecutor.

But what if, despite the active involvement of the United States, a future judge or prosecutor were to fall short of the high standards set by Judges Goldstone, Arbour, and McDonald? First, it is worth noting that it will not be the court's personnel who determine its rules of procedure and evidence or the elements of the crimes to be prosecuted. Those tasks are left to the court's "legislature"—the governments that join the court. The United States, working closely with the world's democracies, is already deeply involved in the process of negotiating and drafting these provisions. I am happy to report that these negotiations have been infused with a commitment to due process and the rule of law.

The court's treaty contains other important checks and balances against overreaching that are similar to, and in some cases more stringent than, those governing American prosecutors and judges. For example, the prosecutor cannot even begin a prosecution without the approval of two separate panels of judges and the possibility of appeal to a third. Moreover, two-thirds of the governments that join the court can remove a judge for misconduct, and a simple majority can remove the chief or deputy chief prosecutor. Far from the "unaccountable" institution that some critics have decried, the International Criminal Court will reflect a separation of powers similar to and be as subject to democratic control as any court in the United States.

Some critics contend that the International Criminal Court would infringe American sovereignty. But there is no sovereign right to commit atrocities, particularly the vicious crimes on which the court would focus. Just as the U.S. Constitution creates a government of limited powers that cannot intrude on basic rights, so international law sets limits to how sovereign governments can treat their own people. It is fully consistent with the American constitutional tradition that genocide and other such crimes be subject to prosecution.

Critics also argue that it would be unconstitutional for the United States to cooperate with the International Criminal Court in the unlikely event that the court sought the surrender of an American. Again, that view is mistaken. To begin with, no treaty, including this one, can compel the United States to violate its Constitution. Moreover, this treaty is fully compatible with our Constitution. The U.S. government routinely enters into extradition treaties with other democracies. At times, we are even required to surrender an American for offenses allegedly committed abroad. The U.S. government agrees to such extradition only when confident that the requesting country can assure a fair trial. Because the International Criminal Court will be governed by the strictest due process standards, there is no constitutional reason why the United States should not cooperate with it in the same way that we cooperate with the courts of our democratic partners. Some have suggested constitutional problems if the International Criminal Court were to seek to prosecute an American for a crime committed on U.S. soil. But the likelihood of U.S. troops committing genocide, war crimes, or crimes against humanity on U.S. soil is too remote for this concern to detain us.

Of course, the International Criminal Court will not look exactly like an American court. For example, there will be no jury. But the same is true of many courts in other democratic countries to which the United States routinely extradites suspects. So long as a fair trial is guaranteed, as it would be with the International Criminal Court, there is no constitutional impediment to U.S. government cooperation.

Despite these safeguards, can I guarantee that the International Criminal Court will never initiate a case against an American? Of course not. No government can or should be able to provide such absolute assurance, for that would be inconsistent with the first principle of justice—that it apply equally to all. But the court's focus on the most heinous crimes, which the United States does not commit, its application of legal standards that are already incorporated into American military doctrine, its deference to good faith investigations and prosecutions by national authorities, and its strict respect for due process provide every reasonable guarantee against the unjustified prosecution of an American.

Moreover, the remote possibility of a frivolous or politically motivated prosecution is vastly outweighed by the court's prospect of promoting justice, deterring tomorrow's tyrants, saving the lives of their countless victims, and minimizing the need for expensive and risky overseas deployments of American troops. As commander in chief of our armed forces, I have the duty to take all possible steps to avoid needlessly risking the lives of the brave men and women who defend our country. I would not relish the sight of an American soldier being brought before the International Criminal Court. But given the many safeguards I have described, I must accept that distant possibility in order to reduce far greater risks to our service members. I could not deploy our troops to stop genocide, and I could not face the parents, spouses, and loved ones of those who might lose their lives in this noble task if I had not done everything in my power to deter such slaughter in the first place. The International Criminal Court is the best tool we have for that purpose.

Some critics attack the court from a different perspective. They fear that it will discourage the international community from coming to the rescue of the victims of mass slaughter, that the Pentagon and our NATO allies would think twice before undertaking a humanitarian mission that might, even theoretically, expose them to criminal prosecution.

But, as I have said, America does not commit genocide, war crimes, or crimes against humanity. Nor do our NATO allies. We do not commit these unspeakable crimes when we are at war, and we certainly do not do so when we act in the name of peace. We thus have nothing to fear from the prosecution of these offenses, nothing to make us hesitate when the pleas of the victims of mass slaughter fill our television screens and their plight hounds our conscience.

Indeed, I am happy to report that these fears were not even voiced when NATO launched air strikes to protect the people of Kosovo from the ruthless forces of Slobodan Milosevic. The Yugoslav War Crimes Tribunal already has jurisdiction over any alleged crime committed by NATO troops in Yugoslavia, just as the International Criminal Court might have jurisdiction over future humanitarian interventions. In fact, unlike the International Criminal Court, the Yugoslav War Crimes Tribunal has the exceptional power to override good faith national investigations and prosecutions. Yet, neither the Pentagon nor our NATO allies hesitated to deploy our military might to stop Milosevic's tyrannical assault on Kosovo's ethnic Albanians.

Some critics argue that because America has assumed special military responsibilities for ensuring world peace, we deserve special privileges, such as an exemption for our soldiers from the jurisdiction of the International Criminal Court. But America does not need or want an exemption to commit atrocities. Any such exemption would undermine the basic principle of justice: that it applies equally to all.

Some contend that the court might prolong suffering by discouraging tyrants from stepping down from power lest they face prosecution. In fact, dictators rarely have the luxury of planning a quiet retirement. They are usually forced to step down because their support wanes. As we saw when Duvalier fled Haiti, when Marcos left the Philippines, when Mengistu fled Ethiopia, when Amin left Uganda, and, most recently, when Suharto resigned as president of Indonesia, failing dictators rarely have the chance to hold out for amnesty from prosecution. When their support fades, their regimes quickly crumble.

Of course, some tyrants plan for their eventual demise by adopting amnesties for their crimes while their grasp on power is still strong. Chile's Pinochet provides a good example. But when the Chilean people rejected his rule in a plebiscite, and major branches of the armed forces stopped supporting his reign, he, too, was forced to resign. Since then, his allies in the armed forces have used the threat of violence to prevent any reexamination of this amnesty. Why should the international community respect such coerced impunity? Indeed, to do so would only encourage further atrocities by suggesting to tomorrow's tyrants that they can use violence and extortion to escape punishment for their crimes.

There are those who say that societies should be free to forget past atrocities and move on without the burden of prosecutions. But because of the coercive powers of dictators, we should be wary of how we characterize the choice of impunity. A choice made with a gun pointed at one's head is not a free choice. To defer to the supposed "national choice" in such circumstances is really to defer to the dictates of the tyrant.

But what if victims freely decide to grant an amnesty, as might be said of South Africa for those abusers who confess fully before its Truth and Reconciliation Commission? In such cases, the International Criminal Court prosecutor might well exercise discretion to defer to this national decision. However, any attempt to move beyond prosecutorial discretion and entrust this matter to a political body will only encourage tyrants to use blackmail to secure their impunity.

Other critics have warned that prosecution by the International Criminal Court might conflict with efforts by the U.N. Security Council to end armed conflict and make peace. If the council were unable to offer combatants an amnesty, they argue, a military leader might feel compelled to keep fighting. In fact, our experience has been the opposite. Take the Dayton Peace Accord for Bosnia. Long before the Dayton Summit, the Yugoslav War Crimes Tribunal issued genocide indictments for Bosnian Serb political and military leaders Radovan Karadzic and Ratko Mladic. That did not stop these leaders from accepting a peace plan, even though the plan did not include an amnesty. Indeed, the indictment of these two accused genocidal killers, by marginalizing them politically and allowing more moderate voices to emerge, made it easier to conclude and implement the Dayton Agreement. Not even Slobodan Milosevic, a man with much blood on his hands, insisted on an amnesty as a price for pulling Serbian forces out of Kosovo.

For similar reasons, these critics want the United States to be able to use its Security Council veto to suspend or block prosecution by the International Criminal Court while peace is being negotiated. The court's treaty does give the Security Council the power to halt court proceedings if the council feels that prosecution might imperil efforts to make peace. But the council must act in such a case as it usually does, by the vote of 9 of its 15 members and the acquiescence of all 5 permanent council members. It would be wrong, as these critics propose, to allow any one permanent member—whether it be the United States, Britain, France, Russia, or China—to stop a prosecution single-handedly in the name of the Security Council. It is not in our interest to allow such a perversion of the council's regular voting procedure.

Some opponents of the ICC take umbrage at the fact that U.S. citizens might fall subject to the court's jurisdiction even if the Senate refuses to ratify its treaty. But the United States routinely extends antiterrorism and antihijacking treaties to the citizens of states that have not ratified them. To do otherwise would be to allow renegade governments to immunize their citizens from prosecution by simply refusing to ratify these anticrime treaties. We thus must accept that other governments can extend the reach of their anticrime treaties to U.S. citizens. But even then, as I have noted, Americans would still be unlikely ever to appear before the International Criminal Court because the United States does not commit genocide, war crimes, or crimes against humanity, and we would prosecute any rogue soldier who did commit such an offense. For similar reasons, there is no need to object to the extension of certain privileges, such as the right to opt out of all war crimes prosecutions for an initial seven years, only to governments that have joined the court. Those incentives to ratification do not endanger American interests.

Some critics fear that the court might someday be empowered to prosecute the crime of aggression. They worry that America might not come to the rescue of those in need if our intervention might be characterized as aggressive rather than humanitarian. But the delegates gathered in Rome did not settle on a definition of aggression. The court will be empowered to consider this crime only if seven-eighths of the governments that join the court agree on a definition. If there is no agreement, prosecution for aggression will not be allowed. The only conceivable definition that could secure such broad support would make prosecution dependent on a finding by the U.N. Security Council that a specific military action was aggressive. In that case, the United States, through its veto in the Security Council, would be able to prevent any inappropriate finding of aggression. Moreover, in the extraordinarily unlikely event that a definition of aggression was arrived at that did not defer to the Security Council's determination, the court's rules would allow any government that had joined the court, including the United States, to reject that definition and thus to block any prosecution of its nationals for that crime.

There have also been objections to the way the court's statute handles the war crime of transferring an occupying state's own population into occupied territory. The Rome negotiators added language to this prohibition in the Geneva Conventions to clarify that for the International Criminal Court it would be a crime if such transfers were done "directly or indirectly." Some fear that this broad formulation might implicate Israeli citizens for their role in encouraging the settlement of the West Bank and Gaza Strip. That contention is debatable. But even if Israelis were in jeopardy of prosecution, Israel could easily avoid that risk by not ratifying the court's treaty, and the United States could use its veto to prevent the Security Council from ordering any unwarranted prosecution despite Israel's lack of ratification. This fear thus provides no reason for the United States itself to refrain from joining the court.

Finally, some critics suggest that because the court is not perfect, the United States should try to renegotiate the treaty. The United States played an important role in shaping the court during the Rome negotiations, but as in every negotiation, we did not gain everything we wanted. After the many compromises already made, our partners are in no mood to reopen the negotiations just because we want a better deal. For the United States to insist on further changes as the price of supporting the court would be to isolate our country from our closest allies and risk damaging our standing and reputation as a strong defender of law and justice.

The court agreed to in Rome is a good one. It protects and advances America's national interest. It will proceed with or without the United States. But it will be a better court with the United States. It is in our interest that we join it.

In sum, there are strong reasons for the United States to embrace the International Criminal Court. By bringing the most egregious criminals to justice and deterring others from repeating their crimes, the court will help promote a lawful and stable international order, answer the pleas of victims, reinforce the ideals on which our nation was founded, and protect the lives of our soldiers. While no new venture is ever risk free, the court's treaty contains ample safeguards against misuse.

When the history books are written on the twentieth century, there will be much misery and cruelty to record. We will never be able to erase the barbarity that has marred so much of our lifetime. Let us at least ensure that the final chapter is dedicated to the eradication of this evil. Rather than submit to this cruelty, let us end the century by pledging to overcome it, by reaffirming our commitment to justice and the rule of law. Let us leave a legacy for which our children will be thankful. Let us insist on giving meaning to our vow of "Never Again!" Let us move forward together, the democratic nations of the world, to build an International Criminal Court. I am proud that America will lead this march.

SPEECH TWO: REJECT AND OPPOSE THE INTERNATIONAL CRIMINAL COURT

John Bolton

My fellow Americans:

I welcome this opportunity to discuss with you my position on the International Criminal Court.

After deep and serious reflection and extensive consultation on a bipartisan basis, I have reconsidered the Statute of Rome. I affirm today that I find it to be a pernicious and debilitating agreement, harmful to the national interests of the United States. We are dealing here with nothing less than America's place in the world. And I can assure you that my highest international priority will be to keep America free and secure. That includes, in my view, strictly adhering to my oath of office to "preserve, protect, and defend the Constitution of the United States" against ill-advised and dangerous multilateral agreements.

I take my oath seriously, and I can promise you that my administration will do nothing internationally to threaten either our Constitution or the sound principles on which it rests. Moreover, I will remain steadfast in preserving the independence and flexibility that America's military forces need to defend our national interests around the world. There are those who wish to limit that flexibility, but they will find no friends in this administration. Let me explain how the ICC's deleterious design would wound and potentially cripple our Constitution and, ultimately, our independence.

In the eyes of its supporters, the ICC is simply an overdue addition to the family of international organizations, an evolutionary step beyond the Nuremberg Tribunal and the next logical institutional development over the ad hoc war crimes courts in Bosnia and Rwanda. The Statute of Rome both establishes substantive principles of international law and creates new institutions and procedures to adjudicate these principles. Substantively, the statute confers jurisdiction on the ICC over four crimes: genocide, crimes against humanity, war crimes, and the crime of aggression. The court's jurisdiction is "automatic," applicable to individuals accused of crimes under the statute whether or not their governments have ratified it. Particularly important here is the independent prosecutor, who is responsible for conducting investigations and prosecutions before the court. The prosecutor may initiate investigations based on referrals by states who are parties to the agreement or on the basis of information that he or she otherwise obtains. While the Security Council may refer matters to the ICC or order it to cease a pending investigation, the council is precluded from a meaningful role in the court's work.

So described, one might assume that the ICC is simply a further step in the orderly march toward the peaceful settlement of international disputes, a step sought since time immemorial. But in several respects the court is poised to assert authority over nation-states and to promote the exclusivity of prosecution over alternative methods for dealing with the worst criminal offenses, whether occurring in war or through arbitrary domestic power. I reject both objectives.

In fact, the court and the prosecutor are illegitimate. The ICC does not fit into a coherent international "constitutional" design that delineates clearly how laws are made, adjudicated, and enforced, subject to popular accountability and structured to protect liberty. There is no such design. Instead, the court and the prosecutor are simply "out there" in the international system. This approach is clearly inconsistent with, and constitutes a stealth approach to eroding, American standards of structural constitutionalism. That is why I view this issue as, first and foremost, a liberty question.

This failing stems from the power purportedly vested in the ICC to create authority outside of (and superior to) the U.S. Constitution and thereby to inhibit the full constitutional autonomy of all three branches of the U.S. government and, indeed, of all states party to the statute. Advocates rarely assert publicly that this result is central to their stated goals, but it must be for the court and prosecutor to be completely effective. And it is precisely for this reason that, strong or weak in its actual operations, this court has unacceptable consequences for the United States.

The court's flaws are basically two-fold: substantive and structural. As to the former, the ICC's authority is vague and excessively elastic. This is most emphatically *not* a court of limited jurisdiction. Even for genocide, the most notorious crime among the four specified in the Statute of Rome, there is hardly complete clarity on its meaning.

Our Senate, for example, cannot accept the statute's definition of genocide unless it is prepared to reverse the position it took in February 1986 in approving the Genocide Convention of 1948. At that time, the Senate attached two reservations, five understandings, and one declaration. By contrast, Article 120 of the Statute of Rome provides explicitly and without any exceptions that "no reservations may be made to this Statute." Thus, confronted with the statute's definition of "genocide" that ignores existing American reservations to the underlying Genocide Convention, the Senate would not have the option of attaching those reservations (or others) to any possible ratification of the Rome Statute. Unable to make reservations to the statute, the United States would risk expansive and mischievous interpretations by a politically motivated court. Indeed, the "no reservations" clause is obviously directed against the United States and its protective Senate. It is a treaty provision no American president should *ever* agree to.

Two other offenses addressed in the Statute of Rome—war crimes and crimes against humanity—are even vaguer, as is the real risk that an activist court and prosecutor can broaden their language essentially without limit. It is precisely this risk that has led our Supreme Court to invalidate state and federal criminal statutes that fail to give adequate notice of exactly what they prohibit under the "void for vagueness" doctrine. Unfortunately, "void for vagueness" is almost solely an American shield for civil liberties. It is my clear duty not to allow that shield to be weakened by the encroachment of international agreements that abridge our constitutional safeguards.

A fair reading of the treaty, for example, leaves me unable to answer with confidence whether the United States would have been considered guilty of war crimes for its bombing campaigns over Germany and Japan in World War II. Indeed, if anything, a straightforward reading of the language probably indicates that the court *would* find the United States guilty. A fortiori, these provisions seem to imply that the United States would have been guilty of a war crime for dropping atomic bombs on Hiroshima and Nagasaki. This is intolerable and unacceptable.

The list of ambiguities goes on and on. How will these vague phrases be interpreted? Who will advise that a president is unequivocally safe from the retroactive imposition of criminal liability after a wrong guess? Is even the defensive use of nuclear weapons a criminal violation? We would not use such weapons except in the direst circumstances, but it would not serve our vital national security interest in deterring aggression to encumber our strategic decisions with such legalistic snares.

Numerous prospective "crimes" might be added to the statute. Many were suggested at Rome and commanded wide support from participating nations. Most popular was the crime of "aggression," which was included in the statute but not defined. Although frequently easy to identify, aggression can at times be in the eye of the beholder. For example, Israel justifiably feared during the negotiations in Rome that its preemptive strike in the Six Day War almost certainly would have provoked a proceeding against top Israeli officials. Moreover, there is no doubt that Israel will be the target of a complaint in the ICC concerning conditions and practices by the Israeli military in the West Bank and Gaza. The United States, with continuous bipartisan support for many years, has attempted to minimize the disruptive role that the United Nations has all too often played in the Middle East peace process. We do not now need the ICC interjecting itself into extremely delicate matters at inappropriate times. That is why Israel voted with the United States against the statute.

Thus, in judging the Statute of Rome, we should not be misled by examining simply the substantive crimes contained in the final document. We have been put on very clear notice that this list is illustrative only and just the start. The fundamental problem with the latitude of the court's interpretative authority stems from the danger that it will evolve in a decentralized and unaccountable way. While the historical understanding of customary international law was that it grew out of the practices of nation-states over long years of development, today we have theorists who write approvingly of "spontaneous customary international law." This is simply not acceptable to any person who values freedom.

The idea of "international law" sounds comfortable to citizens of countries such as ours, where we actually do live by the rule of law. In truth, however, this logic is naive, often irrelevant to the reality of international relations, and in many instances simply dangerous. It mistakes the language of law for the underlying concepts and structures that actually permit legal systems to function, and it seriously misapprehends what "law" can realistically do in the international system. In common sense terms, "law" is a system of rules that regulates relations among individuals and associations, and between them and sources of legitimate coercive authority that can enforce compliance with the rules. The source of coercive authority is legitimate to the extent that it rests on popular sovereignty. Any other definition is either incoherent or intolerable to anyone who values liberty.

To have real law in a free society, there must be a framework—a constitution—that defines government authority and thus limits it, preventing arbitrary power. As the great scholar C. H. McIlwain wrote, "All constitutional government is by definition limited government." There must also be political accountability through reasonably democratic popular controls over the creation, interpretation, and enforcement of the laws. These prerequisites must be present to have agreement on three key structures: authoritative and identifiable sources of the law for resolving conflicts and disputes; methods and procedures for declaring and changing the law; and the mechanisms of law interpretation, enforcement, execution, and compliance. In international law, essentially none of this exists.

Particularly important for Americans, of course, is how all of this applies to us. Proponents of international governance see the United States as the chief threat to the new world order they are trying to create. Small villains who commit heinous crimes can kill individuals and even entire populations, but only the United States can neutralize or actually thwart the new world order itself. Under our Constitution, any Congress may, by law, amend an earlier act of Congress, including treaties, thus freeing the United States unilaterally of any obligation. In 1889, the Supreme Court made this point explicitly in the *Chae Chan Ping* case:

> A treaty . . . is in its nature a contract between nations, and is often merely promissory in its character, requiring legislation to carry its stipulations into effect. Such legislation will be open to future repeal or amendment. If the treaty operates by its own force . . . , it can be deemed in that particular only the equivalent of a legislative Act, to be repealed or modified at the pleasure of Congress. In either case the last expression of the sovereign will must control.

If treaties cannot legally "bind" the United States, it need not detain us long to dismiss the notion that "customary international law," the source of possible new offenses for the ICC to consider, has any binding legal effect either.

We must also understand some facts of international political life. If the American citadel can be breached, advocates of binding international law will be well on the way toward the ultimate elimination of the nation-state. Thus, it is important to understand why America and its Constitution would have to change fundamentally and irrevocably if we accepted the ICC. This constitutional issue is not simply a narrow, technical point of law, certainly not for the United States. I proclaim unequivocally the superior status of our Constitution over the claims of international law. Those who disagree must explain to the people of America how the world's strongest and freest representative democracy, simply by adhering to its own Constitution, somehow contravenes international law.

As troubling as the ICC's substantive and jurisdictional problems are, the problems raised by the statute's main structures—the court and the prosecutor—are still worse. We are considering, in the prosecutor, a powerful and necessary element of executive power, the power of law enforcement. Never before has the United States been asked to place any of that power outside the complete control of our national government. My main concern is not that the prosecutor will target for indictment the isolated U.S. soldier who violates our own laws and values, and his or her military training and doctrine, by allegedly committing a war crime. My main concern is for our country's top civilian and military leaders, those responsible for our defense and foreign policy. They are the real potential targets of the ICC's politically unaccountable prosecutor.

Unfortunately, the United States has had considerable experience in the past two decades with "independent counsels," and that depressing history argues overwhelmingly against international repetition. Simply launching massive criminal investigations has an enormous political impact. Although subsequent indictments and convictions are unquestionably more serious, a zealous independent prosecutor can make dramatic news just by calling witnesses and gathering documents, without ever bringing formal charges.

Indeed, the supposed "independence" of the prosecutor and the court from "political" pressures (such as the Security Council) is more a source of concern than an element of protection. Independent bodies in the U.N. system, such as UNESCO, have often proven themselves more highly politicized than some of the explicitly political organs. True political accountability, by contrast, is almost totally absent from the ICC.

The American concept of separation of powers, imperfect though it is, reflects the settled belief that liberty is best protected when, to the maximum extent possible, the various authorities legitimately exercised by government are placed in separate branches. So structuring the national government, the framers believed, would prevent the excessive accumulation of power in a limited number of hands, thus providing the greatest protection for individual liberty. Continental European constitutional structures do not, by and large, reflect a similar set of beliefs. They do not so thoroughly separate judicial from executive powers, just as their parliamentary systems do not so thoroughly separate executive from legislative powers. That, of course, is entirely their prerogative and substantially explains why they appear to be more comfortable with the ICC's structure, which closely melds prosecutorial and judicial functions in the European fashion. They may be able to support such an approach, but we will not.

In addition, our Constitution provides that the discharge of executive authority will be rendered accountable to the citizenry in two ways. First, the law enforcement power is exercised only through an elected president. The president is constitutionally charged with the responsibility to "take Care that the Laws be faithfully executed," and the constitutional authority of the actual law enforcers stems directly from the president, who is the only elected executive official. Second, Congress, all of whose members are popularly elected, both through its statute-making authority and through the appropriations process, exercises significant influence and oversight. When necessary, the congressional impeachment power serves as the ultimate safeguard.

In European parliamentary systems, these sorts of political checks are either greatly attenuated or entirely absent, just as with the ICC's central structures, the court and prosecutor. They are effectively accountable to no one. The prosecutor will answer to no superior executive power, elected or unelected. Nor is there any legislature anywhere in sight, elected or unelected, in the Statute of Rome. The prosecutor and his or her not-yet-created investigatory, arresting, and detaining apparatus are answerable only to the court, and then only partially. The Europeans may be comfortable with such a system, but that is one reason why they are Europeans and we are not.

Measured by long-standing American principles, the ICC's structure utterly fails to provide sufficient accountability to warrant vesting the prosecutor with the statute's enormous power of law enforcement. Political accountability is utterly different from "politicization," which we can all agree should form no part of the decisions of either prosecutor or court. Precisely contrary to the proper alignment, however, the International Criminal Court has almost no political accountability *and* carries an enormous risk of politicization. This analysis underscores that our main concern is not the isolated prosecutions of individual American military personnel around the world. It has everything to do with our fundamental American fear of unchecked, unaccountable power.

Beyond the particular American interests adversely affected by the ICC, we can and we should worry about the more general deficiencies of the ICC that will affect all nations. Thus, although the gravest danger from the American perspective is that the ICC will be overbearing and unaccountable, it is at least equally likely that in the world at large the new institution will be powerless and ineffectual. While this analysis may sound superficially contradictory, the ICC is ironically one of those rare creations that may be simultaneously dangerous and weak because much of its intellectual underpinning is so erroneous or inadequate.

The most basic error is the belief that the ICC will have a substantial, indeed decisive, deterrent effect against the perpetration of grievous crimes against humanity. Rarely, if ever, however, has so sweeping a proposal had so little empirical evidence to support it. The evidence demonstrates instead that the court and the prosecutor will not achieve their central goal because they do not, cannot, and should not have sufficient authority in the real world.

Behind their optimistic rhetoric, ICC proponents have not a shred of evidence supporting their deterrence theories. In fact, they fundamentally confuse the appropriate roles of political and economic power, diplomatic efforts, military force, and legal procedures. No one disputes that barbarous measures of genocide and crimes against humanity are unacceptable. But it would be a grave error to try to transform international matters of power and force into matters of law. Misunderstanding the appropriate roles of force, diplomacy, and power in the world is not just bad analysis but bad policy and potentially dangerous.

Recent history is filled with cases where even strong military force or the threat of force failed to deter aggression or the commission of gross abuses of human rights. ICC proponents concede as much when they cite cases where the "world community" has failed to pay adequate attention or failed to intervene in time to prevent genocide or other crimes against humanity. The new court and prosecutor, it is said, will now guarantee against similar failures.

But this is surely fanciful. Deterrence ultimately depends on perceived effectiveness, and the ICC fails badly on that point. Even if administratively competent, the ICC's authority is far too attenuated to make the slightest bit of difference either to the war criminals or to the outside world. In cases where the West, in particular, has been unwilling to intervene militarily to prevent crimes against humanity as they were happening, why would a potential perpetrator feel deterred by the mere possibility of future legal action? A weak and distant court will have no deterrent effect on the hard men like Pol Pot who are most likely to commit crimes against humanity. Why should anyone imagine that bewigged judges in The Hague will succeed where cold steel has failed? Holding out the prospect of ICC deterrence to the truly weak and vulnerable is simply a cruel joke.

Beyond the predictive issue of deterrence, it is by no means clear that "justice" is everywhere and always consistent with the attainable political resolution of serious political and military disputes, whether between or within states. It may be, or it may not be. Human conflict teaches that, unfortunately, mortal policymakers often must make trade-offs among inconsistent objectives. This can be a painful and unpleasant realization, confronting us as it does with the irritating facts of human complexity, contradiction, and imperfection. Some choose to ignore these troubling intrusions of reality, but an American president does not have that luxury.

The existing international record of adjudication is not encouraging. Few observers argue that the International Court of Justice (ICJ)—the so-called World Court—has garnered the legitimacy sought by its founders in 1945. This is more than ironic because much of what was said then about the ICJ anticipates recent claims by ICC supporters. These touching sentiments were not borne out in practice for the ICJ, which has been largely ineffective when invoked and more often ignored in significant international disputes. Indeed, after the ICJ's erroneous Nicaragua decisions, the United States withdrew from its mandatory jurisdiction, and the World Court has even lower public legitimacy here than does the rest of the United Nations.

Among the several reasons why the ICJ is held in such low repute, and what is candidly admitted privately in international circles, is the highly politicized nature of its decisions. Although ICJ judges supposedly function independently of their governments, their election by the U.N. General Assembly is thoroughly political, involving horse trading among and within the United Nations' several political groupings. Once elected, the judges typically vote along highly predictable national lines except in the most innocuous of cases. We do not need a repetition of that hypocrisy.

Although supposedly a protection for the ICC's independence, the provisions for the "automatic jurisdiction" of the court and the prosecutor are unacceptably broad. They constitute a clear break from the World Court's basic premise that there is no jurisdiction without the consent of the state parties. Because parties to the ICC may refer alleged crimes to the prosecutor, we can virtually guarantee that some will, from the very outset, seek to use the court for political purposes.

Another significant failing is that the Statute of Rome substantially minimizes the Security Council's role in ICC affairs. In requiring an affirmative council vote to *stop* a case, the statute shifts the balance of authority from the council to the ICC. Moreover, a veto by a permanent member of such a restraining council resolution leaves the ICC completely unsupervised. This attempted marginalization of the Security Council is a fundamental *new* problem created by the ICC that will have a tangible and highly detrimental impact on the conduct of U.S. foreign policy. The Security Council now risks having the ICC interfere in its ongoing work, with all of the attendant confusion between the appropriate roles of law, politics, and power in settling international disputes. It seriously undercuts the role of the five permanent members of the council and radically dilutes their veto power. I will never accept such a change.

More broadly, accumulated experience strongly favors a case-by-case approach, politically and legally, rather than the inevitable resort to adjudication contemplated by the ICC. Circumstances differ, and circumstances matter. Atrocities, whether in international wars or in domestic contexts, are by definition uniquely horrible in their own times and places.

For precisely that reason, so too are their resolutions unique. When the time arrives to consider the crimes, that time usually coincides with events of enormous social and political significance: negotiation of a peace treaty, restoration of a "legitimate" political regime, or a similar milestone. At such momentous times, the crucial issues typically transcend those of administering justice to those who committed heinous crimes during the preceding turbulence. The pivotal questions are clearly political, not legal: How shall the formerly warring parties live with each other in the future? What efforts shall be taken to expunge the causes of the previous inhumanity? Can the truth of what actually happened be established so that succeeding generations do not make the same mistakes?

One alternative to the ICC is the kind of Truth and Reconciliation Commission created in South Africa. In the aftermath of apartheid, the new government faced the difficult task of establishing and legitimizing truly democratic governmental institutions while dealing simultaneously with earlier crimes. One option was widespread prosecutions against the perpetrators of human rights abuses, but the new government chose a different model. Under the commission's charter, alleged offenders came before it and confessed past misdeeds. Assuming they confessed truthfully, the commission in effect pardoned them from prosecution. This approach was intended to make public more of the truth of the apartheid regime in the most credible fashion, to elicit thereby admissions of guilt, and then to permit society to move ahead without the prolonged opening of old wounds that trials, appeals, and endless recriminations might bring.

I do not argue that the South African approach should be followed everywhere or even necessarily that it was correct for South Africa. But it is certainly fair to conclude that that approach is radically different from the International Criminal Court, which operates through vindication, punishment, and retribution (and purportedly deterrence).

It may be that, in some disputes, neither retribution nor complete truth telling is the desired outcome. In many former communist countries, for example, citizens are still wrestling with the legacy of secret police activities of the now-defunct regimes. So extensive was the informing, spying, and compromising in some societies that a tacit decision was made that the complete opening of secret police and Communist Party files will either not occur or will happen with exquisite slowness over a very long period. In effect, these societies have chosen "amnesia" because it is simply too difficult for them to sort out relative degrees of past wrongs and because of their desire to move ahead.

One need not agree with these decisions to respect the complexity of the moral and political problems they address. Only those completely certain of their own moral standing and utterly confident of their ability to judge the conduct of others in excruciating circumstances can reject the amnesia alternative out of hand. Experience counsels a prudent approach that does not invariably insist on international adjudication instead of a course that the parties to a dispute might themselves agree on. Indeed, with a permanent ICC one can predict that one or more disputants might well invoke its jurisdiction at a selfishly opportune moment and thus, ironically, make an ultimate settlement of the dispute more complicated or less likely.

Another alternative, of course, is for the parties themselves to try their own alleged war criminals. Indeed, there are substantial arguments that the fullest cathartic impact of the prosecutorial approach to war crimes and similar outrages occurs when the responsible population itself comes to grips with its past and administers appropriate justice. ICC advocates usually disregard this possibility. They pay lip service to the doctrine of "complementarity," or deference, to national judicial systems, but like so much else connected with the ICC, it is simply an assertion, unproven and untested. In fact, if "complementarity" has any real substance, it argues against creating the ICC in the first place or, at most, creating ad hoc international tribunals. Indeed, it is precisely in the judicial systems that the ICC would likely supplant that the international effort should be made to encourage the warring parties to resolve questions of criminality as part of a comprehensive solution to their disagreements. Removing key elements of the dispute, especially the emotional and contentious issues of war crimes and crimes against humanity, undercuts the very progress that these peoples, victims and perpetrators alike, must make if they are ever to live peacefully together.

Take Cambodia. Although the Khmer Rouge genocide is frequently offered as an example of why the ICC is needed, proponents of the ICC offer feeble explanations for why the Cambodians should not themselves try and adjudicate alleged war crimes. To create an international tribunal for the task implies the incurable immaturity of Cambodians and paternalism by the international community. Repeated interventions, even benign ones, by global powers are no substitute for the Cambodians' coming to terms with themselves.

ICC advocates frequently assert that the histories of the Bosnia and Rwanda tribunals established by the Security Council demonstrate why such a permanent court is necessary. The limited and highly unsatisfactory experience with ad hoc tribunals proves precisely the contrary. Bosnia is a clear example of how a decision to detach war crimes from the underlying political reality advances neither the political resolution of a crisis nor the goal of punishing war criminals. ICC proponents complain about the lack of NATO resolve in apprehending alleged war criminals. But if not in Bosnia, where? If the political will to risk the lives of troops to apprehend indicted war criminals did not exist there, where will it suddenly spring to life on behalf of the ICC?

It is by no means clear that even the Bosnia tribunal's "success" would complement or advance the political goals of a free and independent Bosnia, the expiation of wartime hostilities, or reconciliation among the Bosnian factions. In Bosnia, there are no clear communal winners or losers. Indeed, in many respects the war in Bosnia is no more over than it is in the rest of the former Yugoslavia. Thus, there is no agreement, either among the Bosnian factions or among the external intervening powers, about how the War Crimes Tribunal fits into the overall political dispute or its potential resolution. There is no serious discussion about Bosnia conducting its own war crimes trials. Bosnia shows that insisting on legal process as a higher priority than a basic political solution can adversely affect both justice and politics.

In short, much of the Yugoslav war crimes process seems to be about score settling rather than a more disinterested search for justice that will contribute to political reconciliation. If one side believes that it is being unfairly treated and holds that view strongly, then the "search for justice" will have harmed Bosnian national reconciliation. This is a case where it takes only one to tango. Outside observers might disagree with this assessment, but the outside observers do not live in Bosnia.

The experience of the Rwanda War Crimes Tribunal is even more discouraging. Widespread corruption and mismanagement in that tribunal's affairs have led many simply to hope that it expires quietly before doing more damage. At least as troubling, however, is the clear impression many have that score settling among Hutus and Tutsis—war by other means—is the principal focus of the Rwanda tribunal. Of course it is. And it is delusional to call this "justice" rather than "politics."

Although disappointed by the outcome in Rome, the United States had hoped to obtain sufficient amendments to allow American participation in a modified ICC. However, comprehensive evaluation of the ICC Statute shows that it cannot be squared with either our Constitution or our interests.

Whether the International Criminal Court survives and flourishes depends in large measure on the United States. I believe it should be scrapped. We will, therefore, ignore it in our official policies and statements and attempt to isolate it through our diplomacy, in order to prevent it from acquiring any further legitimacy or resources. The U.S. posture toward the ICC will be "three noes": no financial support, directly or indirectly; no collaboration; and no further negotiations with other governments to "improve" the ICC. Such a policy cannot entirely eliminate the risks posed by the ICC, but it can go a long way in that direction.

I plan to say nothing more about the ICC during the remainder of my administration. I have, however, instructed the secretary of state to raise our objections to the ICC on every appropriate occasion, as part of our larger campaign to assert American interests against stifling, illegitimate, and unacceptable international agreements. The plain fact is that additional "fixes" over time to the ICC will not alter its multiple inherent defects, and we will not advocate any such efforts. We will leave the ICC to the obscurity it so richly deserves.

The United States has many other foreign policy instruments to utilize that are fully consistent with our values and interests. My goals will rest on the concepts named in the two broad avenues that frame our national Mall: Independence and Constitution. Signatories of the Statute of Rome have created an ICC to their liking, and they should live with it. We will not.

SPEECH THREE: IMPROVE THE INTERNATIONAL CRIMINAL COURT

Ruth Wedgwood

My fellow Americans:

Places such as Racak, Srebrenica, and Kigali were once unknown to most Americans. They are small towns and cities, where plain people tried to earn a living and raise their families. They were off the beaten path, not featured in any tour books.

But in the last ten years, these places have flashed onto our television screens and lingered in our memories, for one sad reason—they were the sites of terrible massacres.

In each town, men committed unthinkable acts. Their governments exploited a background of racial, religious, or political hatred to persuade ordinary people to kill without mercy and betray their own souls.

In 1994, in the country of Rwanda in the Great Lakes region of Africa, over 800,000 Tutsi men, women, and children were killed by knife and machete—in churches, bus stations, and sports stadiums, in every gathering place that in ordinary times is a place of community. In the capital city of Kigali, over 100,000 Tutsi were murdered in the space of a few weeks.

In 1995, the same story unfolded in Bosnia. In the fighting between Serbs and Muslims in that strikingly beautiful country, the city of Srebrenica was placed under siege by Serb forces. When the city fell, 7,000 Muslim men were marched to the outskirts and were summarily executed. American spy satellites detected the fresh ground where their bodies were buried in hastily dug mass graves. It was a pathetic attempt to cover up the evidence of a blatant crime. Even afterwards, the graves were disrupted in an attempt to scatter the remains.

More recently, in January 1999, in the province of Kosovo in the former Federal Republic of Yugoslavia, a farming village called

Racak was destroyed—the houses burned, livestock slaughtered, and families killed—in the conflict between Serbs and Albanians in that once remote place. International monitors found 58 bodies, cold as stone. The later actions of the Belgrade government, forcing over 800,000 people to flee for their lives to neighboring countries, are well known to all of us. There were many Racaks.

The interest of the United States in these events stems from the kind of people we are. America is a nation of immigrants, and we haven't forgotten the lands from which we came. America is also a nation of freedom and tolerance, and we have not given up on the ideal of a society in which people of different backgrounds can live peaceably together.

American soldiers fought their way up the boot of Italy and across the fields of France in the Second World War to defeat a fascist regime that stood for the opposite view. We toppled Adolf Hitler and held his government accountable for how it had abused the peoples of Europe, including the Jewish community.

It is now more than 50 years since the trials at Nuremberg, Germany, after the conclusion of the Second World War. The war crimes trials conducted by U.S. Supreme Court Justice Robert Jackson and his colleagues at Nuremberg aimed to prove that individuals must obey some basic moral laws—that a criminal regime masquerading as a government cannot claim ultimate loyalty. Governments exist to serve their citizens, not to abuse them. As the New World descendants of a failed European order, Americans vowed to show the world that the idea of liberty would triumph. The leaders of Hitler's criminal regime, responsible for the deaths of millions, were tried and punished. In the Pacific as well, war crimes trials were held to show to the world the contemptible behavior of the Japanese government.

These trials were intended to give some measure of justice to the victims. The proof put in evidence by trained lawyers, assessed by objective judges, helped to reeducate the peoples of the aggressor regimes, showing what was done in their name by criminal governments.

The United States has taken a leadership role in creating an international safety net of human rights law. Eleanor Roosevelt championed the Universal Declaration of Human Rights in a vote in the U.N. General Assembly in 1948. The United States helped to draft the Genocide Convention, and a Polish immigrant named Raphael Lemkin, teaching at an American law school, coined the very word "genocide" to describe the attempt to kill a whole people. The United States has also worked on the U.N. treaty guarantees of human rights—the International Covenant on Civil and Political Rights and the International Covenant on Economic and Social Rights—and supported the work of the U.N. Human Rights Committee and the Human Rights Commission.

The American military has been a leader in trying to establish respect for the rule of law and the protection of civilians in wartime. The protections of the Geneva Conventions of 1949—for the wounded, shipwrecked, civilians, and prisoners of war—have been made a part of standard military doctrine in our NATO alliance and taught around the globe in America's cooperative security relationships. The United States has pioneered the role of military lawyers as close advisers to operational commanders, showing how military campaigns can be successfully waged while minimizing as much as possible incidental damage to civilian lives, homes, and economic livelihoods. The United States has attempted to stop the proliferation of weapons of mass destruction, such as biological and chemical weapons, that threaten indiscriminate harm against civilian populations.

It is a part of who we are, as Americans, to respond to moral challenge, to try our best to prevent the repetition of moral transgression, and to avoid a cynical acquiescence in the world as it is.

One of our most principled efforts has been the attempt to create individual responsibility for violations of the laws of war. Nuremberg is a living memory, and, faced with the terrible events in the former Yugoslavia and Rwanda, Americans have worked to bring to justice the cynical leaders who ruined their own peoples.

In 1992, Secretary of State Lawrence Eagleburger forthrightly stated that the Serbian regime in Yugoslavia was led by men who were war criminals. In 1993, the United States acted on that view by voting in the Security Council of the United Nations to create an International War Crimes Tribunal for the Former Yugoslavia. This international criminal court sits in the Netherlands, in the famous city of The Hague. Its current president is a distinguished American, Judge Gabrielle Kirk McDonald, a former federal district judge from Houston, Texas, who has led the tribunal with vigor and has written distinguished opinions on questions of jurisdiction, gathering evidence, and the nature of duress. The court's first prosecutor was a fabled South African, Justice Richard Goldstone, who earlier helped to lead South Africa through its transition to democracy and who put the international tribunal on its feet.

The United States worked hard in the United Nations to win funding and backing for the Yugoslav tribunal, overcoming the skepticism of many countries. We proved at Dayton that peace could be brought to Bosnia even while indictments were pending against Serb leaders Radovan Karadzic and General Ratko Mladic.

Slowly and steadily, NATO and U.N. forces in Bosnia have arrested important suspects under indictment by the tribunal, including the mayor of Vukovar, who ordered the cold-blooded killing of 200 patients from a local hospital in eastern Slavonia. The Yugoslav tribunal has arrested General Radislav Krstic for the massacre at Srebrenica. It has tried and convicted a Serb camp guard, Dusko Tadic, for the torture and murder of Muslim prisoners at the Omarska concentration camp in Bosnia. It has indicted defendants such as "Arkan the Tiger"—a Serb paramilitary leader who conducted brutal ethnic cleansing in the Bosnian town of Brcko at the outset of the Bosnian war and who reappeared in Kosovo in 1999 to carry out his deadly work again. And, most dramatically, at the peak of diplomatic activity to end the war in Kosovo, the court announced indictments of Yugoslav President Slobodan Milosevic and several associates.

The Yugoslav tribunal has been evenhanded, recently indicting three Croat generals for their role in the bombardment of the town of Knin in the Serb Krajina during the 1995 Croatian counteroffensive against the Serbs. It is currently conducting the trial of a Croat general, Tihomir Blaskic, for the violent ethnic cleansing of villages in central Bosnia in 1993. It has brought charges against violators from the Serb, Croat, and Muslim communities, wherever the evidence led.

The United States has strongly supported the Yugoslav tribunal with contributions exceeding $15 million annually, the loan of top-ranking investigators and lawyers from the federal government, the support of NATO ground forces in Bosnia and in Kosovo to permit the safe exhumation of graves, and even the provision of U-2 surveillance photographs to locate the places where the nationalist Serb government has tried to hide the evidence of its wrongdoing. The United States, with its European allies, ended the slaughter in Bosnia in 1995 by intervening with NATO troops to implement the Dayton Peace Accord. Since 1995, it has acted in support of the tribunal to assure that, whether in Bosnia or later in Kosovo, the killers of women, children, and noncombatant men do not scoff at the law in the future.

In 1994, the United States also responded to the terrible events in Rwanda by persuading the Security Council to create an International War Crimes Tribunal for Rwanda. The logistical difficulties of that court have been publicized. Its trials must be conducted in Arusha, Tanzania, where security can be assured, while its investigations are carried out in the still unstable environment of Rwanda itself. But the Rwanda Tribunal has scored singular successes with the convictions for genocide of the former prime minister of Rwanda, Leonard Kambunda, and the mayor of Taba, Jean Paul Akayesu.

The Rwanda tribunal has been another high-priority project for the United States, with American financial contributions exceeding $8 million per year and the loan of skilled law enforcement personnel such as Haitian-American prosecutor Pierre Prosper. The Federal Bureau of Investigation arrested a former minister, Elizaphan Ntakirutimana, a Hutu war crimes suspect who fled from Rwanda to Texas. He was wanted for allegedly taking part in the cold-blooded slaying of several dozen Tutsi villagers in a church in Mugonero. The U.S. Department of Justice has vigorously prosecuted the extradition proceedings to complete the surrender of Ntakirutimana to tribunal authorities.

Is this enough? That is the question we now face. Rwanda and the former Yugoslavia are, unfortunately, not the only places where governments will abuse their citizens and where insurgent paramilitaries and government thugs beyond control will prey on civilians. The recent examples of Sierra Leone, the Democratic Republic of the Congo, and the Sudan, as well as the familiar tyranny of Saddam Hussein in Iraq, come to mind.

For these new crises, ad hoc–ism may not work. Attempting to create another new and independent court from the bottom up—for each new episode of genocide and war crimes, for each new inconceivable instance of crimes against humanity—brings a number of serious problems.

Ad hoc–ism doesn't work because, for starters, we can no longer be sure of winning the day in the U.N. Security Council. The tribunals for the former Yugoslavia and Rwanda were created by votes of the council during a cooperative political period. In the honeymoon after the end of the Cold War, vetoes in the council were not a frequent problem. Our Cold War adversaries, Russia and China, who wield veto power as permanent members of the council, were willing to create these tribunals in the common interest.

But the war in Kosovo reminds us that traditional sympathies can also block action in the Security Council. NATO was forced to act in armed defense of Albanian refugees in Kosovo without an updated council decision because Russia stymied further council action. China has also recently shown that narrow issues on a national agenda can block necessary action by refusing to extend the preventive deployment of U.N. peacekeepers in the former Yugoslav Republic of Macedonia on the specious grounds that they were no longer needed. In truth, China was angry at Macedonia because that government had recognized Taiwan. The self-indulgent nature of such action was no bar to China, for Beijing blocked the Macedonian mission just before the war in Kosovo exploded.

As it happens, the existing Yugoslav tribunal will be able to hear war crimes cases from Kosovo because Kosovo is a part of the former Yugoslavia. But the Security Council's failure to act in this serious war drives home the lesson that we can't always count on having an ad hoc solution.

Our many friends and allies in the world have also noticed that a key institution such as a war crimes tribunal is best footed on the solid foundation of state consent. An international court created through the voluntary membership of states will enjoy a strong political legitimacy. Joining the court will stimulate a debate in each of those countries about the nature of a government's obligations toward its citizens.

For better or worse, the limited membership of the Security Council has also become a matter of public excitement in the United Nations. There is less will to use council authority to create new institutions. We will attempt to use the Security Council when necessary, but many countries think permanent ad hoc–ism is unwise.

There are other problems with using ad hoc tribunals each time the need arises. It amounts to starting over with a blank piece of paper, with inevitable delays to build or adapt a courthouse, to hire personnel, and to begin operations. There are recurring legal problems in international prosecutions, such as how to blend common law and civil law legal systems, how to protect witnesses and victims, and how to execute sentences in cooperating countries. These can be systematically worked on over time in a permanent court.

The greatest American statesmen of the last half century—men such as Dean Acheson, who created NATO, and the founders of the Bretton Woods institutions—understood the importance of durable architecture. A generation that enjoys the blessings of a period of relative peace must use its good fortune to create the structures that will contain and mitigate future conflicts. The transience of ad hoc alliances is not sufficient for all future occasions. This is not a step toward world government—far from it, it is the self-interested action of the United States to win allies who will support its highest ambitions for a prosperous and stable security system.

That is why in 1994 the United States joined other countries in proposing a permanent International Criminal Court. We began the process in a legal body of experts called the International Law Commission, where we were ably represented by Ambassador

Robert Rosenstock, a legal counselor who has served in four presidential administrations. A draft statute for a permanent criminal court was put forward that year by the International Law Commission, with firm American support.

Since 1994, the United States and its NATO allies have been engaged in diplomatic talks with the other members of the United Nations to discuss and resolve issues concerning the nature of such a permanent court, including what crimes it should prosecute, how cases should be started, how to guarantee full procedural safeguards, and how the court should relate to national justice systems.

These have been intricate negotiations, in which experts from the Department of Justice, the Department of State, and the Department of Defense have joined together to discuss American views with our foreign friends.

The five years of negotiation came to an important crossroads in Rome in June and July 1998. In a five-week diplomatic conference, our delegation, led by Ambassador David Scheffer, worked around the clock to create the best possible court.

The U.S. delegation worked painstakingly on many important issues, such as a careful definition of international crimes to accord with the traditional fighting doctrine of the American military. We sought ironclad assurances of full due process and a practical jurisdiction for the court. In that work, the delegation was assisted by American church and civic groups who made suggestions, educated foreign governments, and informed the public. In addition, the negotiators drew on the vital input of the American military, which has led the world in showing how careful military planning and the professional education of soldiers can reduce the burdens that war places on innocent civilians.

The negotiations over the last five years have required the expertise of criminal lawyers and military planners as well as diplomats. The talks have, for the most part, not been prominent in public view, perhaps because the design of a tribunal statute requires a scrupulous and detailed analysis of the interplay of its working parts. Any treaty text that is signed by this administration will be subject to the careful review of the U.S. Senate. Legislation to implement its provisions will also be reviewed by the House of Representatives.

The United States will continue to seek the use of ad hoc tribunals when they are appropriate. We have sought an ad hoc tribunal for Cambodia to prosecute the leadership of the Khmer Rouge for their unprecedented "autocide" during the 1970s. We have sought an ad hoc tribunal to hear evidence against Iraqi president Saddam Hussein for his genocide against Kurdish villagers in the north of Iraq and Shia Marsh Arabs in the south of Iraq, and for his war crimes in Kuwait during the Persian Gulf War.

But we must continue to work for a permanent court for the future.

Many important things were accomplished at Rome in the 1998 negotiations. A draft treaty was completed to create a permanent International Criminal Court for the prosecution of systematic war crimes, genocide, and crimes against humanity.

The Rome negotiators wisely avoided overwhelming the court with additional dockets, such as international narcotics or terrorism. Narcotics smuggling has been effectively prosecuted by national courts, and it is a high-volume industry that would exceed any imaginable capacity of an international court. Narcotics traffickers also try to corrupt every institution that opposes them. It would have jeopardized the integrity of the new court to take this tiger by the tail. So, too, a definition of terrorism was too elusive to include in any agreement for the International Criminal Court. The strong latticework of antiterrorism treaties created in the 1970s—to protect aircraft against hijacking and bombing, to protect diplomats, and, recently, to prevent terrorist bombings and nuclear terrorism—has depended on national courts for enforcement, and, so far, the results have been promising.

The Rome negotiators wisely kept their eye on the ball and focused the new International Criminal Court on the key offenses of war crimes, crimes against humanity, and genocide.

In a great victory against some resistant states, American negotiators settled the court's jurisdiction over war crimes in civil wars—making clear that basic standards of humanity must be observed in internecine civil strife as well as in international conflicts. We have had no civil war in this country since the nineteenth century. But many countries are continuously torn by merciless fighting, and the toll on civilians has been high. As UNICEF has noted, 90 percent of the victims in recent wars have been civilians. The application of the law within exploding states displeased some regimes but was key to an effective court.

In addition, all combatants are subject to the same rules of humanity. A private paramilitary leader can be prosecuted if he directs his men to rampage through a village, even though he does not hold public office. The most horrible violations have been committed by insurgent and rebel groups as much as by governments. Insurgents too often use attacks against civilians as a way to shake confidence in the legal government, adamantly arguing that terrorism is a "poor man's weapon." The draft treaty completed at Rome will allow the prosecution of private paramilitaries and insurgent political leaders, as well as miscreant governments.

The Rome negotiations also accomplished America's purpose of codifying and clarifying modern humanitarian law. For example, systematic crimes against humanity can now be prosecuted whether or not they occur during wartime. This closes the loophole left open at Nuremberg, when Joseph Stalin narrowed the definition of crimes against humanity to exclude his creation of a prison gulag. The millions of political prisoners in the former Soviet Union would have testified that crimes against humanity can indeed occur during times of ostensible peace. Under the Rome Treaty, Joseph Stalin can no longer rest in peace.

The Rome negotiations also made clear that systematic rape and sexual assault are war crimes. The criminal practice in the Bosnian war of forcing Muslim women to bear children fathered by their rapists is condemned for its violation of human dignity. The Vatican and women's groups came to a mutually agreeable formulation that condemned rape, sexual slavery, enforced prostitution, enforced sterilization, and any unlawful confinement of a woman made pregnant with the intent of affecting the ethnic composition of a population.

The important idea of command responsibility was incorporated in the Rome Statute. American military doctrine holds that a commander must control the conduct of his troops in the field. That is a fundamental tenet of professional soldiering and good order. The law of command responsibility establishes that a superior officer is criminally liable if he fails without excuse to monitor the actions of his troops and to punish misconduct. The Rome Statute also applies the idea of command responsibility to civilians, holding that a civilian leader is complicit if he consciously disregards information that the troops under his control are abusing civilians.

So, too, Rome affirms the Nuremberg principle that public office is not a law unto itself. The privilege of public office does not immunize a person from responsibility under the laws of war. The Genocide Convention and the statutes of the Rwanda and Yugoslav tribunals affirm that even a head of state is bound by the basic standards of human rights and may be liable if he commits war crimes, crimes against humanity, or genocide. Office would not protect Adolf Hitler or Pol Pot—or Slobodan Milosevic.

These were signal achievements, and our Rome team can be proud of its accomplishments. But other important benchmarks were created at Rome as well. The Rome Statute incorporates a number of features that the United States valued to protect its own national security interests.

First, Rome provides for "complementarity," the idea that the primary responsibility for enforcing the law of war must remain with each nation-state and with national military justice systems. A case can be brought by the International Criminal Court only when a national justice system is unwilling or unable to proceed with a good faith disposition of the matter. The prosecutor is obliged to notify the national authorities if he or she proposes to open a case, and the national justice system is allowed to take priority over the case unless it is acting in bad faith. The prosecutor's decision to go forward is subject to challenge in a pretrial chamber of the tribunal and to an additional appeal. (These are, incidentally, safeguards that the Congress never thought to provide in the U.S. Independent Counsel Act.)

On another point of concern, the Rome Statute provides complete protection for sensitive national security information. The treaty calls on participating nations to make available to the court the evidence that is necessary for prosecution and defense of criminal cases. But the disclosure of classified information can never be compelled by the court. The United States will share information to the extent that we can without compromising sources and methods needed to monitor ongoing security problems. The protection of intelligence sources and methods is of prime importance in the fight against terrorism and the fight against the proliferation of weapons of mass destruction. We will never compromise on this issue, and the Rome Statute has sagely agreed that this decision must remain in our hands.

Isolated incidents of military misconduct that occur in wartime will not be prosecuted by the court. Rather, the tribunal is charged to focus on war crimes committed "as part of a plan or policy" or as part of "a large-scale commission of such crimes." This assures that the court will not waste its time on the occasional misconduct that national justice systems should handle on their own. It is designed, instead, to focus on countries where the regime itself has become a criminal actor.

A soldier is trained to obey all lawful orders. To protect soldiers from unfair prosecution the Rome Treaty provides for a "superior orders" defense. Only where an order was "manifestly unlawful" can a case against a military subordinate be proposed.

The Rome Statute also respects our bilateral treaty agreements protecting American troops stationed abroad against any attempted exercise of foreign criminal jurisdiction—the so-called Status of Forces Agreements, or SOFAs. Under these agreements, American forces cannot be arrested or prosecuted by foreign authorities without the consent of the United States. SOFA agreements protect all the NATO forces stationed throughout Europe. In addition, the working arrangement of U.N. peacekeeping missions also leaves military discipline to the decisions of the troops' own national government. Although a binding interpretive statement of the Rome Preparatory Commission may be advisable to avoid any ambiguity, the Rome Treaty has been read by the conference chairman to preserve and respect all SOFA agreements— even against the jurisdiction of the International Criminal Court, thus immunizing American soldiers, sailors, airmen, and marines from any exercise of local or ICC criminal justice authority in the countries where they are stationed. Even in countries where we don't have a formal SOFA treaty, the working arrangement with local authorities should be considered an international agreement respected by the Rome Statute. In any case entertained by the International Criminal Court, a demand for arrest would have to be served on the United States directly, and the president would then make a decision how to proceed.

There was much good work done at Rome. We can celebrate how far we have journeyed in the creation of an effective International Criminal Court.

The work is not finished, however. Just as the Rome Conference was preceded by four years of preparatory work, the treaty text voted last July is not a complete work that can stand alone. It is due to be followed by several more years of negotiations on crucial issues such as defining the specific elements of criminal offenses, the specific rules of procedure, and the binding rules of evidence. These negotiations are designed to assure parties that the crucial working parts of the tribunal are known in advance, rather than leaving them to the less certain decisions of judges. Thus, we will not know the shape of the entire package of Rome until this work is complete.

Our government will continue work on the landmark process of putting meat on the bare bones of the treaty text. It is my hope that this process can eliminate several ambiguities in the treaty text that prevent the United States from immediately signing the treaty. There were times in the intense pace of the five-week conference at Rome when our friends and partners did not seem to understand the full range of American security concerns, but in conversations since that time many of our friends have shown the earnest desire to fix what is wrong with the treaty package.

Let me explain what those problems are, and how we propose to resolve them. We hope to keep working with our friends and allies to improve the Rome package, so that the time may come when we can join the permanent court as a full member.

It is clear that the United States is in a unique posture in the world. We have 200,000 troops deployed abroad. We provide the backbone for peacekeeping and peace enforcement operations, since we are the only power with the ability to provide global intelligence, logistics, and airlift. We must be capable of resisting aggressive powers, anywhere around the globe, countering the Saddam Husseins of the world, by maintaining a ready force. We will lead the fights against the proliferation of weapons of mass destruction and against terrorism, even when that requires us to act alone and in controversial circumstances. We will continue to maintain the freedom of navigation necessary to a world commercial power by conducting freedom of navigation exercises and disputing excessive maritime claims by a number of states. We will, when circumstances permit, reverse human rights violations such as the ethnic cleansing in Kosovo carried out by Slobodan Milosevic. We are not afraid to be strong, and we are not afraid to act alone.

We are also not naive. We understand that in a world of realpolitik, a number of countries may attempt to misuse the mechanism of the court. They will not have any practical chance of success, but they may attempt to score political points by filing complaints and referring matters for investigation.

For this reason, there are a number of binding interpretations of the Rome Treaty that we need to secure from our colleagues in the Preparatory Commission before we can contemplate signature of the statute. We will never compromise our security, and we will continue to approach the Rome enterprise with full realism, even while attempting to strengthen international law enforcement against atrocities and massacres.

First, we need the assurance that in our targeting decisions we are never required to share sensitive information. We recently used Tomahawk cruise missiles to destroy the al Shifa pharmaceutical plant in the Sudan. We were convinced that this plant was misused by the government of Sudan and the terrorist network of Osama bin Laden in the attempt to acquire chemical weapons. This was a disputed military action because the plant also had some civilian functions, but it was one we judged necessary for the protection of U.S. security interests. The bin Laden terrorist network is too dangerous for any compromise in our fight against it.

The necessary latitude for good faith military judgments can be protected in the Rome Statute. We hope to obtain a binding interpretation from the Rome Preparatory Commission, through its construction of the elements of offenses, that a targeting decision based on sensitive intelligence sources will be respected. The tribunal should accept a solemn representation by the U.S. government that it possessed a well-grounded basis for believing a target was legitimate—for example, when the target was a chemical weapons transshipment point—without any disclosure of intelligence sources and methods.

Second, to protect our policy judgments on the use of force, we plan to ask our Rome colleagues for a binding interpretation that there is a protected sphere for good faith military decisions. No military action should be challenged unless it was "manifestly unlawful." This is important because there are justifiable differences over how countries interpret the law of self-defense. The practical application of self-defense has changed over the years and will continue to change. We adjust and revise our military rules of engagement to reflect these nuances in conflicts of varied natures.

For example, during the Somalia peacekeeping mission we declared that so-called technical vehicles would be considered presumptively hostile—these were truck-mounted automatic weapons manned by Somalian militias considered too dangerous to allow in the vicinity of our troops. Similarly, in our air and naval operations, we urge our personnel to be "forward leaning"—not to take the first hit but rather to anticipate threats. They are entitled to fire in self-defense when they perceive either a hostile act or a demonstration of hostile intent (such as energizing a fire-control radar), or a force that is declared hostile in an ongoing engagement. These actions of self-defense are, in our judgment, necessary and proportionate.

To protect the right of self-defense, we will ask our Rome colleagues to recognize that the court must defer to any military action that is not "manifestly unlawful." Good faith differences in military doctrine should be argued in military journals and the public press, not in a criminal courtroom.

This is a European idea as well as an American doctrine. The Europeans recognize the idea of deference to national practice in the venerable policy of "margin of appreciation." Even if the International Criminal Court disagrees with a particular decision, it would not be entitled to act unless the decision fell outside any conceivable lawful judgment. A massacre of civilians in cold blood at Racak would fall outside the margin of appreciation. The suppression of integrated air defense systems by disabling an electrical grid would be protected as an appropriate instance of a commander's judgment.

This same idea of a "zone of good faith" judgment has been used in our domestic law to protect police officials in situations where the law is changing. Since the United States often functions as a last resort police force abroad, it is appropriate for it to have the same protection.

There is a third important interpretation of the treaty text that we will seek from our Rome colleagues. This concerns amendments of the text and the reach of those amendments. Article 121 (5) provides that any future change in the tribunal's jurisdiction will not affect treaty parties that vote against the change. We wish to make clear that states that have not yet signed up for the Rome Court are also immune from the effect of jurisdictional amendments.

We care about this because some countries have proposed to add the crime of aggression to the court's jurisdiction. American prosecutors presented the case of aggression against Nazi Germany at the Nuremberg trials in 1945. However, we are skeptical of adding this category of crime to the workload of the International Criminal Court because of its potential for misuse by adversaries in disputed judgments about the use of force abroad. Yugoslavia claims, for example, that NATO actions in Kosovo are "aggression." At a minimum, it is necessary to preserve the exclusive authority of the Security Council to decide what constitutes aggression before a case goes forward—and in that forum, the United States will wisely exercise its veto. Preserving an opt-out provision for countries that have not voted in favor of a change in the court's jurisdiction, including nontreaty parties, will also provide the necessary protection for the United States.

In addition, we need to be sure that countries that stay outside the treaty cannot use the court opportunistically. Article 12 (3) of the Rome Treaty allows a nonparty to agree to jurisdiction "with respect to the crime in question" in a particular matter. If a rogue country is contemplating use of the court to challenge an action of the United States, we wish to make clear that the acceptance of the court's jurisdiction will also apply to that country's own actions. Saddam Hussein has no standing to bring a complaint about Allied enforcement actions against his country unless he is willing to accept scrutiny of his own actions in killing the Kurds in the north and the Marsh Arabs in the south. We doubt that Saddam will accept the challenge.

We hope as well that our Rome colleagues will agree to a limited reading of Article 12 in regard to the court's assertion of jurisdiction over third parties to the treaty. An advantage of the Rome Treaty over ad hoc tribunals created by the Security Council is that it founded the exercise of jurisdiction on the keystone of state consent. It thus makes no sense to take an expansive view of jurisdiction over nationals whose states have not yet acceded to the treaty. The court can always act in situations involving nonparties where the matter has been referred to the court by the Security Council. That will be sufficient for most cases. Where the council hasn't acted, there is no reason to allow the assertion of third party jurisdiction over situations stemming from multilateral peacekeeping or peace enforcement, or where the acts are adopted as the "official acts" of a U.N. member. This is an exception to jurisdiction, not to the underlying rules of the laws of war, and it is designed to allow a country to take time in assessing the work of the tribunal before deciding whether to join.

This is consistent with the sensible provision that allows even a treaty party to wait seven years—in a "transition" period— before joining the court's jurisdiction over war crimes. If treaty parties can wait seven years, it is only reasonable to allow nonparties the same courtesy for a preparatory period.

Finally, we need to have assurances concerning the protection of Israel and its role in the Middle East peace process. The definition of serious violations of the laws and customs of war in the Rome Statute should make clear that the prohibition of transferring a civilian population into an occupied territory "directly or indirectly" extends no further than the existing Geneva Conventions. As scholars have noted, the Rome Statute explicitly limits the court's jurisdiction to violations "which are within the established framework of international law." But as an additional safeguard, the United States has offered language in the Preparatory Commission to restrict the reach of the provision on the voluntary transfer of population to situations where the transfer "endangers the separate identity of the local population." This will avoid any misuse of the court's jurisdiction to harry the question of settlements in the Middle East peace process, which must be left to negotiation between the parties.

It is my hope that all Americans will come to support the work of the International Criminal Court. It serves our highest purposes. Through the binding interpretations just described, which we will seek in the proceedings of the Rome Preparatory Commission, American security interests will be fully protected. The court needs American support, for without us its orders will be disregarded and its mandates spurned. The International Criminal Court will be our partner in working through challenges to international security and in accepting referrals through the Security Council to prosecute any foreign thugs who disregard the rights of their own people and threaten their neighbors.

Our policy will be to cooperate with the court as a nonparty while working to bring about those changes that will permit the United States eventually to adhere formally to the Rome Statute.

I count on the court to seek a close relationship with the enlightened militaries of the world and to rely on them for expert witnesses and advice and even for the necessary education in the evolution of the law of war and international humanitarian law. The American military has been the strongest partner of international humanitarian work on the ground in difficult conflict areas. Members of the military and of the humanitarian community work side by side in remote places where people are in need. This close working relationship will flourish at the International Criminal Court as well.

We also look forward to helping the court identify the best possible men and women to serve as its judges, prosecutors, and defense lawyers. Given time, the International Criminal Court can establish a record that gives confidence to democratic members of the international community, showing that it has sensible priorities, high craftsmanship in its decisions, and a rigorous sense of due process. We have been strong supporters of the ad hoc tribunals for Rwanda and the former Yugoslavia. I have no doubt that, over time, we will become the strongest supporter of the International Criminal Court.

With a project so historically significant as the International Criminal Court, it would ill become America to stand with the naysayers. We did not say "no" to NATO. We did not say "no" to Bretton Woods. And we are well on the way to an International Criminal Court that deserves "yes" for an answer. We will continue working with our partners to make this court an institution that fully accommodates the important role of the United States in enforcing the rule of law. We owe it to the people of Bosnia, Rwanda, and Kosovo. We owe this work to all Americans as well, for we are a people of faith and justice.

BACKGROUND MATERIALS

APPENDIX A

U.S. OBJECTIONS TO THE ROME STATUTE OF THE INTERNATIONAL CRIMINAL COURT

In a statement before the Committee on Foreign Relations of the U.S. Senate on July 23, 1998, just after the conclusion of the Rome Conference, Ambassador Scheffer listed the following objections to the International Criminal Court (ICC) Statute negotiated and approved in Rome:

- Fundamental disagreement with the parameters of the ICC's jurisdiction: Article 12 of the Statute establishes jurisdiction (absent a Security Council referral) when either the state on whose territory the crime was committed is a party or when the accused person's state of nationality is a party. The U.S. delegation argued that this jurisdiction was both too broad and too narrow. Ambassador Scheffer, noting that a great number of recent atrocities have been committed by governments against their own people, stated that under Article 12 construction a state could simply stay a non-party and remain outside the reach of the ICC. At the same time, a non-party, e.g., the United States, participating in a peacekeeping force in a state party's territory, could be subject to ICC jurisdiction. Moreover, because a non-party cannot opt out of war crimes jurisdiction for the permitted seven years, its exposure may be even greater than that of state parties.

- Desire for an "opt out" provision: Ambassador Scheffer indicated that the United States was unsuccessful in obtaining a broad ability for states to "opt out" of ICC jurisdiction for up to 10 years. During that time, he argued, states, particularly the United States, could evaluate the ICC and determine if it was operating effectively and impartially. Under Article 124, the Statute does allow a seven year opt-out period for war crimes.

- Opposition to a self-initiating prosecutor: the United States objects to the establishment of a prosecutor with independent power to initiate investigations without either referral from a state party or the Security Council.

- Disappointment with the inclusion of an undefined "crime of aggression": Traditionally, a crime of aggression is what the Security Council determines it to be. The current text provides for ICC jurisdiction over crimes of aggression, but leaves the definition to subsequent amendment. The United States would like to maintain the linkage between a Security Council determination that aggression has occurred and the ICC's ability to act on this crime.

- Displeasure with the Statute's "take it or leave it" approach: Against the urging of the United States, a provision was adopted which prohibits reservations to the Statute. Mr. Scheffer noted his dissatisfaction, stating "we believed that at a minimum there were certain provisions of the Statute, particularly in the field of state cooperation with the court, where domestic constitutional requirements and national judicial procedures might require a reasonable opportunity for reservations that did not defeat the intent or purpose of the Statute."

APPENDIX B

EXCERPTS FROM THE ROME STATUTE OF THE INTERNATIONAL CRIMINAL COURT

Adopted by the United Nations Diplomatic Conference of Plenipotentiaries on the Establishment of an International Criminal Court on 17 July 1998

PREAMBLE

... **Affirming** that the most serious crimes of concern to the international community as a whole must not go unpunished and that their effective prosecution must be ensured by taking measures at the national level and by enhancing international cooperation,

Determined to put an end to impunity for the perpetrators of these crimes and thus to contribute to the prevention of such crimes ...

Determined to these ends and for the sake of present and future generations, to establish an independent permanent International Criminal Court in relationship with the United Nations system, with jurisdiction over the most serious crimes of concern to the international community as a whole,

Emphasizing that the International Criminal Court established under this Statute shall be complementary to national criminal jurisdictions ...

Have agreed as follows:

PART 2
JURISDICTION, ADMISSIBILITY AND APPLICABILITY

Article 5
Crimes within the Jurisdiction of the Court

1. The jurisdiction of the Court shall be limited to the most serious crimes of concern to the international community as a whole. The Court has jurisdiction in accordance with this Statute with respect to the following crimes:

   (a) The crime of genocide;

   (b) Crimes against humanity;

   (c) War crimes;

   (d) The crime of aggression.

2. The Court shall exercise jurisdiction over the crime of aggression once a provision is adopted in accordance with articles 121 and 123 defining the crime and setting out the conditions under which the Court shall exercise jurisdiction with respect to this crime. Such a provision shall be consistent with the relevant provisions of the Charter of the United Nations.

Article 11
Jurisdiction ratione temporis

1. The Court has jurisdiction only with respect to crimes committed after the entry into force of this Statute.

2. If a State becomes a Party to this Statute after its entry into force, the Court may exercise its jurisdiction only with respect to crimes committed after the entry into force of this Statute for that State, unless that State has made a declaration under article 12, paragraph 3.

Article 12
Preconditions to the Exercise of Jurisdiction

1. A State which becomes a Party to this Statute thereby accepts the jurisdiction of the Court with respect to the crimes referred to in article 5.

2. In the case of article 13, paragraph (a) or (c), the Court may exercise its jurisdiction if one or more of the following States are Parties to this Statute or have accepted the jurisdiction of the Court in accordance with paragraph 3:

(a) The State on the territory of which the conduct in question occurred or, if the crime was committed on board a vessel or aircraft, the State of registration of that vessel or aircraft;

(b) The State of which the person accused of the crime is a national.

3. If the acceptance of a State which is not a Party to this Statute is required under paragraph 2, that State may, by declaration lodged with the Registrar, accept the exercise of jurisdiction by the Court with respect to the crime in question. The accepting State shall cooperate with the Court without any delay or exception....

Article 13
Exercise of Jurisdiction

The Court may exercise its jurisdiction with respect to a crime referred to in article 5 in accordance with the provisions of this Statute if:

(a) A situation in which one or more of such crimes appears to have been committed is referred to the Prosecutor by a State Party in accordance with article 14;

(b) A situation in which one or more of such crimes appears to have been committed is referred to the Prosecutor by the Security Council acting under Chapter VII of the Charter of the United Nations; or

(c) The Prosecutor has initiated an investigation in respect of such a crime in accordance with article 15.

Article 14
Referral of a Situation by a State Party

1. A State Party may refer to the Prosecutor a situation in which one or more crimes within the jurisdiction of the Court appear to have been committed requesting the Prosecutor to investigate the situation for the purpose of determining whether one or more specific persons should be charged with the commission of such crimes.

2. As far as possible, a referral shall specify the relevant circumstances and be accompanied by such supporting documentation as is available to the State referring the situation.

Article 15
Prosecutor

1. The Prosecutor may initiate investigations proprio motu on the basis of information on crimes within the jurisdiction of the Court.

2. The Prosecutor shall analyse the seriousness of the information received. For this purpose, he or she may seek additional information from States, organs of the United Nations, intergovernmental or non-governmental organizations, or other reliable sources that he or she deems appropriate, and may receive written or oral testimony at the seat of the Court.

3. If the Prosecutor concludes that there is a reasonable basis to proceed with an investigation, he or she shall submit to the Pre-Trial Chamber a request for authorization of an investigation, together with any supporting material collected. Victims may make representations to the Pre-Trial Chamber, in accordance with the Rules of Procedure and Evidence.

4. If the Pre-Trial Chamber, upon examination of the request and the supporting material, considers that there is a reasonable basis to proceed with an investigation, and that the case appears to

fall within the jurisdiction of the Court, it shall authorize the commencement of the investigation, without prejudice to subsequent determinations by the Court with regard to the jurisdiction and admissibility of a case.

5. The refusal of the Pre-Trial Chamber to authorize the investigation shall not preclude the presentation of a subsequent request by the Prosecutor based on new facts or evidence regarding the same situation.

6. If, after the preliminary examination referred to in paragraphs 1 and 2, the Prosecutor concludes that the information provided does not constitute a reasonable basis for an investigation, he or she shall inform those who provided the information. This shall not preclude the Prosecutor from considering further information submitted to him or her regarding the same situation in the light of new facts or evidence.

Article 16
Deferral of Investigation or Prosecution

No investigation or prosecution may be commenced or proceeded with under this Statute for a period of 12 months after the Security Council, in a resolution adopted under Chapter VII of the Charter of the United Nations, has requested the Court to that effect; that request may be renewed by the Council under the same conditions.

Article 17
Issues of Admissibility

1. Having regard to paragraph 10 of the Preamble and article 1, the Court shall determine that a case is inadmissible where:

(a) The case is being investigated or prosecuted by a State which has jurisdiction over it, unless the State is unwilling or unable genuinely to carry out the investigation or prosecution;

(b) The case has been investigated by a State which has jurisdiction over it and the State has decided not to prosecute the person concerned, unless the decision resulted from the unwillingness or inability of the State genuinely to prosecute;

(c) The person concerned has already been tried for conduct which is the subject of the complaint, and a trial by the Court is not permitted ...;

(d) The case is not of sufficient gravity to justify further action by the Court.

2. In order to determine unwillingness in a particular case, the Court shall consider, having regard to the principles of due process recognized by international law, whether one or more of the following exist, as applicable:

(a) The proceedings were or are being undertaken or the national decision was made for the purpose of shielding the person concerned from criminal responsibility for crimes within the jurisdiction of the Court referred to in article 5;

(b) There has been an unjustified delay in the proceedings which in the circumstances is inconsistent with an intent to bring the person concerned to justice;

(c) The proceedings were not or are not being conducted independently or impartially, and they were or are being conducted in a manner which, in the circumstances, is inconsistent with an intent to bring the person concerned to justice.

3. In order to determine inability in a particular case, the Court shall consider whether, due to a total or substantial collapse or unavailability of its national judicial system, the State is unable to obtain the accused or the necessary evidence and testimony or otherwise unable to carry out its proceedings.

PART 5
INVESTIGATION AND PROSECUTION

Article 53
Initiation of an Investigation

1. The Prosecutor shall, having evaluated the information made available to him or her, initiate an investigation unless he or she determines that there is no reasonable basis to proceed under this Statute. In deciding whether to initiate an investigation, the Prosecutor shall consider whether:

   (a) The information available to the Prosecutor provides a reasonable basis to believe that a crime within the jurisdiction of the Court has been or is being committed;

   (b) The case is or would be admissible under article 17; and

   (c) Taking into account the gravity of the crime and the interests of victims, there are nonetheless substantial reasons to believe that an investigation would not serve the interests of justice.

   If the Prosecutor determines that there is no reasonable basis to proceed and his or her determination is based solely on subparagraph (c) above, he or she shall inform the Pre-Trial Chamber.

2. If, upon investigation, the Prosecutor concludes that there is not a sufficient basis for a prosecution because:

   (a) There is not a sufficient legal or factual basis to seek a warrant or summons ...;

   (b) The case is inadmissible under article 17; or

   (c) A prosecution is not in the interests of justice, taking into account all the circumstances, including the gravity of the crime, the interests of victims and the age or infirmity of the alleged perpetrator, and his or her role in the alleged crime;

The Prosecutor shall inform the Pre-Trial Chamber and the State making a referral under article 14 or the Security Council in a case under article 13, paragraph (b), of his or her conclusion and the reasons for the conclusion.

3. (a) At the request of the State making a referral under article 14 or the Security Council under article 13, paragraph (b), the Pre-Trial Chamber may review a decision of the Prosecutor under paragraph 1 or 2 not to proceed and may request the Prosecutor to reconsider that decision.

(b) In addition, the Pre-Trial Chamber may, on its own initiative, review a decision of the Prosecutor not to proceed if it is based solely on paragraph 1 (c) or 2 (c). In such a case, the decision of the Prosecutor shall be effective only if confirmed by the Pre-Trial Chamber.

4. The Prosecutor may, at any time, reconsider a decision whether to initiate an investigation or prosecution based on new facts or information.

Article 54
Duties and Powers of the Prosecutor with Respect to Investigations

1. The Prosecutor shall:

(a) In order to establish the truth, extend the investigation to cover all facts and evidence relevant to an assessment of whether there is criminal responsibility under this Statute, and, in doing so, investigate incriminating and exonerating circumstances equally;

(b) Take appropriate measures to ensure the effective investigation and prosecution of crimes within the jurisdiction of the Court, and in doing so, respect the interests and personal circumstances of victims and witnesses, including age, gender ... and health, and take into account the nature of the crime, in particular where it involves sexual violence, gender violence or violence against children; and

(c) Fully respect the rights of persons arising under this Statute.

2. The Prosecutor may conduct investigations on the territory of a State:

3. The Prosecutor may:

(a) Collect and examine evidence;

(b) Request the presence of and question persons being investigated, victims and witnesses;

(c) Seek the cooperation of any State or intergovernmental organization or arrangement in accordance with its respective competence and/or mandate;

(d) Enter into such arrangements or agreements, not inconsistent with this Statute, as may be necessary to facilitate the cooperation of a State, intergovernmental organization or person;

(e) Agree not to disclose, at any stage of the proceedings, documents or information that the Prosecutor obtains on the condition of confidentiality and solely for the purpose of generating new evidence, unless the provider of the information consents; and

(f) Take necessary measures, or request that necessary measures be taken, to ensure the confidentiality of information, the protection of any person or the preservation of evidence.

PART 11
ASSEMBLY OF STATES PARTIES

**Article 112
Assembly of States Parties**

1. An Assembly of States Parties to this Statute is hereby established. Each State Party shall have one representative in the Assembly who may be accompanied by alternates and advisers. Other

States which have signed the Statute or the Final Act may be observers in the Assembly.

2. The Assembly shall:

   (a) Consider and adopt, as appropriate, recommendations of the Preparatory Commission;

   (b) Provide management oversight to the Presidency, the Prosecutor and the Registrar regarding the administration of the Court;

   (c) Consider the reports and activities of the Bureau established under paragraph 3 and take appropriate action in regard thereto;

   (d) Consider and decide the budget for the Court;

   (e) Decide whether to alter . . . the number of judges;

   (f) Consider . . . any question relating to non-cooperation;

   (g) Perform any other function consistent with this Statute or the Rules of Procedure and Evidence.

3. (a) The Assembly shall have a Bureau consisting of a President, two Vice-Presidents and 18 members elected by the Assembly for three-year terms.

   (b) The Bureau shall have a representative character, taking into account, in particular, equitable geographical distribution and the adequate representation of the principal legal systems of the world.

   (c) The Bureau shall meet as often as necessary, but at least once a year. It shall assist the Assembly in the discharge of its responsibilities.

4. The Assembly may establish such subsidiary bodies as may be necessary, including an independent oversight mechanism for inspection, evaluation and investigation of the Court, in order to enhance its efficiency and economy.

5. The President of the Court, the Prosecutor and the Registrar or their representatives may participate, as appropriate, in meetings of the Assembly and of the Bureau.

6. The Assembly shall meet at the seat of the Court or at the Headquarters of the United Nations once a year and, when circumstances so require, hold special sessions. Except as otherwise specified in this Statute, special sessions shall be convened by the Bureau on its own initiative or at the request of one third of the States Parties.

7. Each State Party shall have one vote. Every effort shall be made to reach decisions by consensus in the Assembly and in the Bureau. If consensus cannot be reached, except as otherwise provided in the Statute:

(a) Decisions on matters of substance must be approved by a two-thirds majority of those present and voting provided that an absolute majority of States Parties constitutes the quorum for voting;

(b) Decisions on matters of procedure shall be taken by a simple majority of States Parties present and voting.

8. A State Party which is in arrears in the payment of its financial contributions towards the costs of the Court shall have no vote in the Assembly and in the Bureau if the amount of its arrears equals or exceeds the amount of the contributions due from it for the preceding two full years. The Assembly may, nevertheless, permit such a State Party to vote in the Assembly and in the Bureau if it is satisfied that the failure to pay is due to conditions beyond the control of the State Party.

9. The Assembly shall adopt its own rules of procedure.

10. The official and working languages of the Assembly shall be those of the General Assembly of the United Nations.

PART 13
FINAL CLAUSES

Article 119
Settlement of Disputes

1. Any dispute concerning the judicial functions of the Court shall be settled by the decision of the Court.

2. Any other dispute between two or more States Parties relating to the interpretation or application of this Statute which is not settled through negotiations within three months of their commencement shall be referred to the Assembly of States Parties. The Assembly may itself seek to settle the dispute or make recommendations on further means of settlement of the dispute, including referral to the International Court of Justice in conformity with the Statute of that Court.

Article 120
Reservations

No reservations may be made to this Statute.

Article 121
Amendments

1. After the expiry of seven years from the entry into force of this Statute, any State Party may propose amendments thereto. The text of any proposed amendment shall be submitted to the Secretary-General of the United Nations, who shall promptly circulate it to all States Parties.

2. No sooner than three months from the date of notification, the next Assembly of States Parties shall, by a majority of those present and voting, decide whether to take up the proposal. The Assembly may deal with the proposal directly or convene a Review Conference if the issue involved so warrants.

3. The adoption of an amendment at a meeting of the Assembly of States Parties or at a Review Conference on which consen-

sus cannot be reached shall require a two-thirds majority of States Parties.

4. Except as provided in paragraph 5, an amendment shall enter into force for all States Parties one year after instruments of ratification or acceptance have been deposited with the Secretary-General of the United Nations by seven-eighths of them.

5. Any amendment to article 5 of this Statute shall enter into force for those States Parties which have accepted the amendment one year after the deposit of their instruments of ratification or acceptance. In respect of a State Party which has not accepted the amendment, the Court shall not exercise its jurisdiction regarding a crime covered by the amendment when committed by that State Party's nationals or on its territory.

6. If an amendment has been accepted by seven-eighths of States Parties in accordance with paragraph 4, any State Party which has not accepted the amendment may withdraw from the Statute with immediate effect, notwithstanding paragraph 1 of article 127, but subject to paragraph 2 of article 127, by giving notice no later than one year after the entry into force of such amendment.

7. The Secretary-General of the United Nations shall circulate to all States Parties any amendment adopted at a meeting of the Assembly of States Parties or at a Review Conference.

Article 122
Amendments to Provisions of an Institutional Nature

1. Amendments to provisions of the Statute which are of an exclusively institutional nature . . . may be proposed at any time . . . by any State Party. The text of any proposed amendment shall be submitted to the Secretary-General of the United Nations or such other person designated by the Assembly of States Parties who shall promptly circulate it to all States Parties and to others participating in the Assembly.

2. Amendments under this article on which consensus cannot be reached shall be adopted by the Assembly of States Parties or by a Review Conference, by a two-thirds majority of States Parties. Such amendments shall enter into force for all States Parties six months after their adoption by the Assembly or, as the case may be, by the Conference.

Article 123
Review of the Statute

1. Seven years after the entry into force of this Statute the Secretary-General of the United Nations shall convene a Review Conference to consider any amendments to this Statute. Such review may include, but is not limited to, the list of crimes contained in article 5. The Conference shall be open to those participating in the Assembly of States Parties and on the same conditions.

2. At any time thereafter, at the request of a State Party and for the purposes set out in paragraph 1, the Secretary-General of the United Nations shall, upon approval by a majority of States Parties, convene a Review Conference.

3. The provisions of article 121, paragraphs 3 to 7, shall apply to the adoption and entry into force of any amendment to the Statute considered at a Review Conference.

Article 124
Transitional Provision

Notwithstanding article 12, paragraph 1, a State, on becoming a party to this Statute, may declare that, for a period of seven years after the entry into force of this Statute for the State concerned, it does not accept the jurisdiction of the Court with respect to the category of crimes referred to in article 8* when a crime is alleged to have been committed by its nationals or on its territory. A declaration under this article may be withdrawn at any time. The pro-

---

* Article 8 defines "war crimes" under the Rome Statute.

visions of this article shall be reviewed at the Review Conference convened in accordance with article 123, paragraph 1.

Article 125
Signature, Ratification, Acceptance, Approval or Accession

1. This Statute shall be open for signature by all States in Rome, at the headquarters of the Food and Agriculture Organization of the United Nations, on 17 July 1998. Thereafter, it shall remain open for signature in Rome at the Ministry of Foreign Affairs of Italy until 17 October 1998. After that date, the Statute shall remain open for signature in New York, at United Nations Headquarters, until 31 December 2000.

2. This Statute is subject to ratification, acceptance or approval by signatory States. Instruments of ratification, acceptance or approval shall be deposited with the Secretary-General of the United Nations.

3. This Statute shall be open to accession by all States. Instruments of accession shall be deposited with the Secretary-General of the United Nations.

Article 126
Entry into Force

1. This Statute shall enter into force on the first day of the month after the 60th day following the date of the deposit of the 60th instrument of ratification, acceptance, approval or accession with the Secretary-General of the United Nations.

2. For each State ratifying, accepting, approving or acceding to the Statute after the deposit of the 60th instrument of ratification, acceptance, approval or accession, the Statute shall enter into force on the first day of the month after the 60th day following the deposit by such State of its instrument of ratification, acceptance, approval or accession.

Article 127
Withdrawal

1. A State Party may, by written notification addressed to the Secretary-General of the United Nations, withdraw from this Statute. The withdrawal shall take effect one year after the date of receipt of the notification, unless the notification specifies a later date.

2. A State shall not be discharged, by reason of its withdrawal, from the obligations arising from this Statute while it was a Party to the Statute, including any financial obligations which may have accrued. Its withdrawal shall not affect any cooperation with the Court in connection with criminal investigations and proceedings in relation to which the withdrawing State had a duty to cooperate and which were commenced prior to the date on which the withdrawal became effective, nor shall it prejudice in any way the continued consideration of any matter which was already under consideration by the Court prior to the date on which the withdrawal became effective.

ABOUT THE AUTHORS

JOHN BOLTON is the Senior Vice President of the American Enterprise Institute. During the Bush Administration, he served as the Assistant Secretary of State for International Organization Affairs, where he was responsible for U.S. policy throughout the U.N. system. In the Reagan Administration, he was the Assistant Attorney General in charge of the Civil Division, the Department of Justice's largest litigating division, where he personally argued several major constitutional law cases.

ALTON FRYE is the Presidential Senior Fellow at the Council on Foreign Relations, where he has also served as President and as National Director. Previously a member of the RAND Corporation and a U.S. Senate staff director, he has taught at UCLA and Harvard. A frequent consultant to Congress and the executive branch, his books include *A Responsible Congress: The Politics of National Security*.

KENNETH ROTH is Executive Director of Human Rights Watch, the largest U.S.-based human rights organization, which he has led for six years. He served previously as a federal prosecutor in New York and in the Iran-Contra investigation. A graduate of Yale Law School and Brown University, Mr. Roth has conducted numerous human rights missions around the world. He has testified frequently before Congress and international bodies and has written extensively on human rights abuses, international justice, and war crimes.

ANNE-MARIE SLAUGHTER is J. Sinclair Armstrong Professor of International, Foreign, and Comparative Law and Director of Graduate and International Legal Studies at Harvard Law School. She writes and teaches on a range of subjects in international law and international relations, including the effectiveness of international tribunals and the relationship between national

government institutions and international organizations. She recently published "The Real New World Order" in the 75th anniver-
sary issue of *Foreign Affairs*.

RUTH WEDGWOOD is Senior Fellow for International Organizations and Law at the Council on Foreign Relations and Professor
of Law at Yale University. In 1998–99, she served as the Stock-
ton Professor of International Law at the U.S. Naval War Col-
lege. She was a law clerk for the U.S. Supreme Court, and a
Federal Prosecutor in the Southern District of New York.